DOCUMENTS OF MODERN HISTORY

General Editor:

A. G. Dickens

The Development of the Welfare State in Britain 1880–1975

J. R. Hay

St. Martin's Press
New York

Library of Congress Cataloging in Publication Data
Hay, J. Roy.
    The development of the welfare state in Britain, 1880–1975.
    Includes bibliographical references.
    1. Great Britain—Social policy—History—Sources. 2. Public
welfare—Great Britain—History—Sources. I. Title.
HN382. H33   361'.941   77–28671
ISBN 0–312–19749–7

Contents

Preface

Many people assisted, sometimes consciously, in the preparation of this book. Pat Thane, Keith Burgess, Bob Holton and Jim Treble provided documents. Nancy Porter, Orla Henry and June Connelly turned scraps of paper and a crabbed script into presentable manuscript. My Glasgow students lived with the ideas and the sources and tried to knock some sense into the author, as did Roger Davidson, Joe Melling and Terry Rogers. Terry Gourvish proved to be the best linkman in the business. My wife, Frances, should by rights receive any credit for the book's appearance, but the responsibility – and the blame – for its defects lies with me.

In the latter stages of compiling the book I received a grant from the Houblon–Norman Fund to continue research on employers and their organizations. Some of the ideas and documents here are the result of that assistance, for which I am extremely grateful.

J. R. Hay
January 1978

Acknowledgements

The Publishers' thanks are due to the following for permission to reproduce copyright material:

Department of Social Administration, London School of Economics for an extract from B. Abel-Smith's and P. Townsend's *The Poor and the Poorest*; Longman Group Ltd for an extract from A. Briggs's *Social Thought and Social Action: A Study of the Work of Seebohm Rowntree*; Times Newspapers Ltd for an extract from R. A. Butler's *The Art of the Possible*; Cassell & Co. Ltd for an extract from Winston Churchill's *The Second World War*, II, *The Hinge of Fate*; Her Majesty's Stationery Office for extracts from Command Paper 3920 (1931) and Command Paper 6405 (1942); Oxford University Press for an extract from *Thomas Jones: Whitehall Diary* edited by Keith Middlemas, I, 1916–25 (1969); Trades Union Congress for extracts from Annual Report (1930) and Memorandum by the TUC, Social Insurance and Allied Services; and George Allen & Unwin Ltd for an extract from R. M. Titmuss's *Commitment to Welfare* and a diagram from A. T. Peacock's and J. V. Wiseman's *The Growth of Public Expenditure in the United Kingdom*.

Introduction

In this book, I have attempted to draw attention to some aspects of the development of the welfare state in Britain since the late nineteenth century. Documentary evidence has been used, where possible, to illustrate and illuminate major issues and the views of the various social groups concerned with social policy and its broader implications for society. Some new areas of study, such as the complex range of views held by members of the working class in regard to state welfare or the influence of employers on the process of social reform, can be illustrated, though not quantitatively demonstrated, by documents with the minimum of supporting comment. On the other hand, the administration of welfare and the relationship between welfare and economic development are less easily presented through documents alone and as a result the last section of the book takes the form rather of a documentary essay in which the relevant issues are placed more specifically and firmly in the context of recent historical debates.

This format may be of greater use to students and teachers alike since it presents assistance to the reader where I believe it is most required, while leaving the more accessible areas of study open to the imagination with the minimum of comment and interpretation. The introduction outlines the content of the major chapters of the book and draws attention to areas of debate, controversy and lack of knowledge.

It is generally accepted that the development of the British welfare state is closely associated with changes in the role and influence of the working class. But though accepted, this is not something which has been seriously studied until very recently and accordingly some very simple views about the relationships between the working class and the welfare state are still popular. It was Sydney Webb as early as 1892 who stated that collectivism, by which term he would have comprehended most aspects of current social policy, was the economic obverse of democracy (1). Since he wrote, many have followed him in believing that the extension of state welfare was an inevitable product of such changes as the spread of the franchise, the rise of trade unions and the Labour Party, with the threat of more violent changes lurking in the background to spur on any reluctant politicians to greater welfare concessions to labour.

Like most simple views there is a little truth in this one; but recent research is demonstrating, first, that working-class attitudes to state welfare were a good deal more complex, sophisticated and ambivalent and, secondly, that working-class influence on the process of social reform was not the sole and simple direct cause of that reform, though it was by no means an insignificant element in the process. The documents in Chapter I therefore have a dual purpose. They attempt to demonstrate some of the range of working-class attitudes to social welfare, taking account of the views of those both within and outside formal organizations. They also indicate, in conjunction with documents in Chapters II, III and IV, the nature and extent of working-class influence on the process of reform.

Some of the reality of poverty in the early years of this century is indicated in the first chapter (6–8, 12), hinting at the ways in which fluctuations in the economy, the decline of particular trades, ill-health, old age or family responsibilities could plunge a family into poverty. The 'awful uncertainty' (52 – this phrase is Churchill's in 1907) of the lives of workers comes out vividly in the sailmaker's appeal to Glasgow Distress Committee in the midst of the 1908–9 depression.

Despite this reality, members of the working class held widely differing views on how best to tackle the causes of poverty. By the early 1900s many were clear as to the potential benefits and the dangers of state intervention (2–4, 9). The leader from the *Foresters' Miscellany* (4) is particularly interesting, coming as it does from one of the largest friendly societies, whose working-class members are often regarded as having identified themselves fully with the individualist self-help ethic of the Victorian middle class. It is clear from this extract that there was a working-class collectivist form of self-help which was subtly, but profoundly, different from the individualist conception of Samuel Smiles, and that this world view did not see the answer to the problem of poverty in state intervention. Research is still needed to determine the relative popularity of these different ideologies. For example, there was a wide range of responses within one trade union to a proposal in the

1890s to establish the eight-hour day by legislation (3). There is also a contrast between the positive case as presented by the trades council of an area of relatively harmonious industrial relations and the syndicalist critique of state welfare (5, 11). The former also shows the links between some trades union bodies and progressive employers on the question of old-age pensions. Organized labour and political labour tended, on the whole, to support welfare legislation (10, 54), though their conception of welfare often went beyond that being put forward by the other parties.

During and immediately after the first world war, industrial unrest, provoked by the effects of inflation, profiteering and some aspects of government policy towards labour, seemed, on occasions, about to spill over into revolutionary agitation (13). To counter this, influential voices within government and the civil service argued for a positive social reform programme (48). However, once the post-war boom broke, deflation and unemployment became the order of the day, and working-class organizations pressing for welfare reform were thrown increasingly on the defensive (67). Aspirations towards more comprehensive and humane social services were never completely lost, but the main concern of the 1920s and 1930s was to resist cuts in the levels of services or benefits (15).

It was not until the outbreak of the second world war that organized labour took the offensive once again. Pressure from labour led to the setting up of the Beveridge Committee (57). The aims of the parliamentary committee of the Trades Union Congress make an interesting comparison with the two sets of employers' views discussed below (16, 31–3). During the war, trade union and Labour Party leaders became members of the government and Cabinet and it is interesting that there is less sign of the discriminating opposition to state welfare common between 1890 and 1920, though this had not entirely disappeared (17). The Beveridge Report was widely accepted by organized labour and, as far as can be judged, by the mass of the people, and Churchill's lukewarm reception of it probably did him considerable political harm (58). Churchill's attitude was very similar to that of the majority of employers (31) who wanted consideration of social reform postponed until after the war. In fact, the implementation of social legislation began towards the end of the war with Butler's Education Act of 1944 (59), which was supported by labour on the whole.

The Labour government's social legislation of 1945–8, which is generally accepted as marking the institution of the welfare state, was the outcome of much of the social planning which had gone on during the second world war. It has often been argued that there was little which was distinctively socialist in these measures and that they owed more to the liberal ideas of Beveridge and Keynes.[1] However, the labour movement, through the Labour Party, had been the most insistent proponent of social reform throughout the war and the fact that the Labour Party had been able to enter and sustain a role in government during the war ensured that the impetus towards reform was never lost, as it might have been.[2]

Since the war, the peculiarly socialist drive for social legislation has been somewhat muted. The rhetoric of income redistribution has been maintained but the Labour government of 1964–70 was unable in practice to bring about any significant change (62). Nevertheless, the 'rediscovery' of poverty among the old and in large or single-parent families by Titmuss, Abel-Smith and the Child Poverty Action Group helped to encourage further reform. A struggle then developed between those who wished to see welfare benefits made universally available and those who wanted resources concentrated on specific groups in need (72–3). The labour movement, on the whole, retaining memories of the dole and the means test, tended to support universal rather than selective services, but the pressures towards selectivity and the maintenance of incentives by keeping welfare benefits below the level of previous earnings, the so-called 'wage stop', remained strong. The labour movement also had to respond to the growth of private welfare schemes, especially pensions, sponsored by employers. In this case it could be argued that the initiative by private employers, taking advantage of tax concessions available since 1921, forced the Labour Party to reconsider its own welfare strategy (60). Inevitably, this raises the question of the relative shares of responsibility for the introduction of social legislation attributable to different groups in society.

If directly exerted pressure by working-class groups and political organizations is insufficient, by itself, to explain the development of social welfare in Britain, then the attitudes and influence of other social groups must be examined. Perhaps the most important, if one of the least studied, groups is employers of labour in industry and commerce. Employers have an interest in welfare both within the firm and as developed by the state. That interest is based on certain common elements in the relationships between employers and labour at all times in a capitalist society, but it is not a static or unchanging interest. Nor is welfare simply a function of the level of economic development in capitalist society, even though the steady growth of social services expenditure in societies like Britain is a remarkable feature (**66**).

In their interest in welfare, employers may be reacting to pressure from the workers. Where workers are calling for specific reforms, employers may offer alternative schemes geared to the needs of capital rather than labour. Alternatively, by offering social benefits and enmeshing the leadership of working-class organizations in welfare institutions, employers may see welfare reforms as a means of undermining general industrial militancy and unrest. Such institutions may offer an alternative to, or a modification of, trade union action. In both cases the motive for welfare is an extension of social control by employers directly or through the medium of the state (**20–21**).

Employers have other reasons for being concerned with welfare. Welfare may be seen as one contribution to the productive efficiency of the firm or of the national economy in a competitive environment. Employers, thus, have an interest in the health, efficiency, resilience and skill of their employees and, more generally, of the working class as a whole from which they draw their labour force. The obverse of efficiency is the cost of social welfare which might, in some circumstances, have to be borne by the employer, though it could often be passed on to the consumer in higher prices, or to the employee through a slower growth of wages, depending on the economic circumstances of the firm. If welfare did produce greater efficiency, of course, this would offset some of the costs involved.

In the early stages of industrialization, where labour skills were vital to the individual firm and labour turnover was often a serious problem, employers tended to prefer internal (that is, internal to a particular firm) welfare schemes, which linked or fettered the worker to the firm, and reinforced the existing incentive system within the firm. Discriminating welfare schemes could be used to reward respectable, hard-working and disciplined employees, while the rough, recalcitrant and inefficient could be ignored or penalized (**18–22**). As enterprises expanded, the economy became more concentrated and interrelated, employers increasingly came to require labour without specific skills, or with skills which could be imparted with relatively less investment provided the worker was basically educated, fit and adaptable. At this stage, external welfare services, with the cost being borne in part by the state, the employee or the customer, appeared more efficient than internal welfare schemes, or an important supplement to them (18, 23). Another reason for the generalizing of welfare schemes through the state might well be to prevent 'unfair' competition by groups of employers who did not provide welfare, but exploited their workers to a greater degree. This was a powerful influence in factory legislation in Britain (19) and the USA.[3]

The meeting point of the motives of social control and economic efficiency is the area of labour discipline. According to employers, welfare within the firm or through the state must contribute to efficiency through improved labour discipline, if it is to be effective (22, 29). Therefore, such welfare measures as were required of the state had to reinforce labour discipline, not weaken it. To employers, welfare might reduce poverty with beneficial effects on consumption, but it had to be part of an efficient manpower policy to gain their support (22, 27, 29).

Given the varying costs and benefits of welfare to employers, it is hardly surprising that employer attitudes to welfare have changed and developed according to the economic and social circumstances they faced. From the late nineteenth century to around 1920, as foreign competition and labour unrest intensified, many influential employers began to argue for state welfare as a means of social control and as a contribution to economic efficiency (21, 27, 28). Even at this time not all were convinced of the benefits of welfare (24, 25). Thereafter, when mass unemployment took the edge off labour militancy and guaranteed a supply of labour, employers became more sensitive to the costs of welfare. In the 1920s and 1930s, they tended to oppose the extension of state welfare (29, 30, 71).

It was not until the second world war that employer attitudes began to change once again, though they remained divided on the main elements of the post-Beveridge welfare programmes (31–3). By this time, industrial concentration was producing larger business units which had greater resources for welfare experiments, and also greater influence, through business organizations, on government policy. Since the war one of the most noticeable features has been the re-growth of internal company welfare schemes, including occupational pension schemes, designed to win the loyalty of employees, particularly white-collar workers, to the firm. Such schemes were now supported by tax concessions rather than a corresponding increase in institutional welfare provision by the state (60). In very recent times, employers have once again been concerned about the costs of public welfare (63).

It is clear, therefore, that employer attitudes and influence on the development of state welfare have been significant. For an earlier period, this influence can be demonstrated, as in the case of labour exchanges and unemployment insurance before 1914 (18–26). But here, as elsewhere, the role of civil servants and other experts in the formulation of policy is important and cannot be reasonably interpreted as solely a response to pressure from workers or employers.

The role of experts and civil servants in making social policy has been the subject of much recent research and controversy. Following the work of MacDonagh on the regulation of conditions aboard emigrant ships, there has been a tendency to emphasize the importance and independence of civil servants in the process of reform. It has been suggested that 'bureaucratic imperatives', forces for expansion from within the civil service itself, resulting from the involvement of officials in administration and drafting of legislation, can account for much of the extent and character of welfare measures. Moreover, it has also been argued that legislation only proceeded when a consensus between officials and experts had been reached and that, accordingly, the stress on the role of politicians or outside pressures, particularly from organized labour, should be reduced. Finally, the officials and experts tended to develop and virtually monopolize the increasing statistical knowledge which, it has been suggested, was the essential prerequisite for social legislation.

Taken together these are powerful arguments, but Chapters I and II illustrate some of the ways in which civil servants and experts were subject to effective pressures. Chapter III, in concentrating on the views and activities of these groups, is an attempt to illustrate the degree and the limitations of the independent contribution of these groups to the process of reform. The first three extracts (34–6) reveal something of the extent of knowledge about poverty before the famous studies of Booth and Rowntree. Booth's massive investigation of conditions in London in the 1880s has been the subject of much recent analysis. Any quotation from this work is bound to be selective but this one does capture some of the similarities of his views to those common in the 1860s and the moral preoccupation of his approach, while still hinting about the change to a more quantitative and systematic analysis of the causes of poverty which was to develop in the next generation (37). Examples of aspects of this concern are taken from the work of Rowntree, who became highly influential in Liberal circles just before and during the first world war, and of Beveridge, who was brought into the Board of Trade by Churchill in 1908 (38, 44).

The introduction of acknowledged experts into the civil service has occurred regularly in Britain but full-time civil servants also played important parts in overall reform. The strategy of Sir Robert Morant in connection with the medical inspection of schoolchildren is an example (42). He also maintained links with the Webbs (43).

During the first world war, civil servants were primarily concerned with labour issues, such as the introduction of 'dilution' – that is removing existing trade union barriers to the recruitment of skilled workmen in order to ensure a sufficient supply of munitions workers, both male and female. However, the vast increase in female employment in factories and the need to sustain high levels of output led to concern over the standards of health and welfare provision. The leading Quaker employer, Seebohm Rowntree, was brought into the Ministry of Munitions to spearhead the campaign for improved health and welfare facilties (27).

After the first world war the prime concern in the civil service, or at least in the Treasury, was to cut back social expenditure, a view reinforced by the Geddes Committee of 1922 (67). In fact, expenditure on social services continued to rise throughout the inter-war period, especially on health services (66), despite the conclusions of the Royal Commission on National Health Insurance of 1926 (30). Some of the increase is explained by demographic changes, some by the consequences of policy decisions made before and during the first world war, and much by the extension of these policies which had been forecast in the earlier period (53). It has been argued that social policy in the 1920s and 1930s was left to the experts and the civil servants. 'Social politics were a matter for private adjustment, for conferences between low-level ministers, their civil servants and lobby delegations.'[4] While it is true that matters of social policy occupied relatively little parliamentary time, it is clear that, when issues of principle came up, mobilization of the political forces was organized.[5] Accordingly, it seems more plausible to consider that the civil servants and experts were operating within limits set by the major policy innovations of the pre-war period. It proved very difficult to cut back social expenditure because of the large contractual element involved and the strong resistance of labour and other vested interests, but bureaucratic independence seldom ran to the implementation of novel departures in social policy.

Very often in social policy, particular issues made headway only when different groups came to see value in that issue for themselves in terms of their own specific interests. So employers and labour and civil servants and politicians might be supporting a superficially similar line of policy, but for entirely different reasons. This is somewhat different from the idea of an emerging consensus. The agreement stretched as far as the area or name of the policy, while the details and the purpose of the policy required by each group remained distinct. The introduction of family allowances, which has been the subject of much recent interest, is a classic case of this type.[6] Family allowances were initially proposed by Eleanor Rathbone as a means of reducing poverty among children in large families. In the 1920s and early 1930s trade unions tended to oppose family allowances for fear of weakening their position in wage bargaining. They preferred higher wages all round rather than sops to reduce poverty. By the late 1930s, however, as unemployment began to fall and the strength and self-confidence of trade unions began to recover, they came round to the view that family allowances could be seen as an addition to wage increases.

Employers on the other hand, some of whom began to pay family allowances within the firm, tended to see family allowances as a means of heading off demands for all round wage increases. Moreover, family allowances would maintain differentials between those in work and those out of work, provided the family responsibilities were similar. Some Conservative politicians and many experts, concerned with the declining birth rate and the possibility of a stagnant or declining population, saw family allowances as a means of stimulating natality, as was being done in France at the time. But what finally brought them into the immediate political agenda was Keynes's appreciation during the second world war that family allowances as an alternative to a general increase in wages could be a means of macro-economic control. If wages were increased generally this would lead to excess demand and inflation. Family allowances would cause much less overall increase in purchasing power, yet deal with the most obvious points of pressure on family incomes.

Proposals for legislative reform had to be accepted finally, of course, by parliament. Few today would accept that politicians or political parties had a completely free hand in the matter of social reform, but the programmes or manifestos of parties and the initiatives of individual politicians were of considerable importance in the process of reform. Chapter IV, accordingly, complements the previous material by illustrating the changing scope of state welfare as seen by the various parties, bringing out, where possible, the similarities and differences between the Conservative, Liberal and Labour conceptions of welfare (51–6). It also tries to indicate the extent of individual initiative by politicians and their personal ideas on welfare (51–3, 58, 59). These views should always be compared with other contemporary extracts to establish the degree to which they were novel and how far they reflected common opinion.

Progressive Liberals and Conservatives shared the view that social legislation was an antidote to socialism or social revolution from the late 1880s onwards (51–3), though some had a somewhat broader conception of welfare. It has been argued that the major parties differed on the means by which social reform was to be achieved. Conservatives did not wish to see a redistribution of income between classes, but preferred that the costs of welfare be borne by classes in proportion to the benefits they received. The Liberals, by contrast, were prepared to countenance a redistribution of income between classes (52, 53, 55). In practice, however, the contributory principle, introduced by the Liberals with the National Insurance Act of 1911 and extended to pensions by the Conservatives in 1925, tended to ensure that the working class, on the whole, paid for its own welfare; in this way such redistribution as took place was within the class, from those in work to those without, from the workers to the old and to the young, from the healthy to the sick, rather than from the rich to the poor (24). Moreover, though progressive income and capital taxes have been extended in Britain since 1896, the total tax burden tends to be proportional to income rather than progressive, even today. While members of the working class, and those with low incomes particularly, receive the bulk of benefits under social security, other welfare benefits, such as education, appear to be used to a greater extent by the middle and upper classes. The extent and nature of income redistribution through welfare and taxation, therefore, remains a highly complex and controversial issue.

The Labour Party had initially a greater commitment to welfare and income redistribution than the Liberals, but while commitment remains (54, 56), it has been modified and, many would say, circumscribed particularly since the second world war. Compare, for example, the aims of the Labour Party manifesto of 1974 (62) and their New Frontiers for Social Security (60) with the health service programme of 1918, or the manifesto from 1900 (56, 54).

One issue which has divided the parties since the second world war has been that of selectivity versus universalism in the social services. Particularly during the period of increasing affluence of the 1960s, many on the right began to argue that comprehensive welfare benefits had outlived their usefulness and that benefits should instead be concentrated on the very poor and special categories of people such as the disabled or the handicapped (73, 74). Criticism from the left took two forms. One approach was to argue that poverty still existed on a considerable scale, which required an extension rather than curtailment of welfare. The other suggested that the discrimination and investigation required for selective benefits would perpetuate a lower class of welfare beneficiaries and would reintroduce the stigma associated with the means test and the dole (73). In recent years these debates have increasingly tended to cut across party lines, and since 1974 supporters of universalist social services have been forced increasingly on to the defensive (63).

To understand how the welfare state operates in practice it is essential to delve below the political rhetoric to examine the administration of the various acts. Quite often the original ideas and intentions of politicians were considerably modified by those, both within the civil service and without, who were involved in the process of administration. At other times the administration of legislation revealed major gaps or deficiencies in the present act and created opportunities and occasionally the dynamic for subsequent modification. The break-up of the Poor Law in the latter part of the nineteenth century and the early part of the twentieth was in part brought about by innovation from within, but there was a fierce struggle between those wanting change and those who wished to adhere to the principles of 1834 (64).[7] The administration of the national health insurance scheme after 1911 clearly demonstrated the extent of illness among women at work who were covered by the act (65). On the other hand, dependent women and children were excluded from benefits under the act and remained so, on the whole, till 1948. For the latter, the only source of assistance was often still the Poor Law, though a few employers and workers' benefit societies were extended to dependants after 1911 (26).

The administration of unemployment insurance in the 1920s has been the subject of a recent valuable study (69). Under the early unemployment insurance acts the amount of benefit obtained was strictly limited by the number of contributions paid (22), but with mass unemployment in the 1920s and 1930s this system broke down. It was replaced by a stipulation that those receiving benefit had to be 'genuinely seeking work' (69). The experience of one American academic who disguised himself as an unemployed workman and attended the courts of referees under the insurance acts is particularly revealing (70).

During the second world war the origins of the Beveridge Report provide another example of initiative from within the civil service.[8] Beveridge himself turned what had been intended as an exercise in coordination and standardization into a comprehensive plan for social reconstruction in the aftermath of the war. On the other hand, the setting up of the committee owed a great deal to pressure from the Trades Union Congress, while there is now considerable debate as to the novelty of the Beveridge proposals. It has been argued that he did little more than systematize and integrate ideas which were common among a wide range of social groups in the period before the war. Furthermore, the measures actually implemented between 1944 and 1948 differed in many important respects from the Beveridge proposals. Nevertheless, even the exercise of linking the different strands of policy may be regarded as an important advance, assisted as it was by needs of wartime morale and social cohesion.

In the 1950s and 1960s the administration of welfare legislation has become even more complex as the range of services and benefits has increased. The relative simplicity of the Beveridge scheme has been superseded by a range of overlapping provisions, whose very complexity has often frustrated both the aspirations of those who sought to deal with social problems and the needs of those who sought the benefits. Many services have a low rate of take-up. Some provisions have resulted in disincentives to work, with marginal tax rates approaching or exceeding one hundred per cent, despite the strenuous efforts of employers and other groups to maintain incentives. The implications and consequences of some of these administrative problems are discussed in Chapter V.

NOTES

1 For a recent discussion, see J. Harris, 'Social Planning in Wartime: Some Aspects of the Beveridge Report', in J. M. Winter (ed.), *War and Economic Development* (Cambridge, 1975), 239–56.

2 P. Addison, *The Road to 1945* (1975).

3 See, for example, A. J. Lea, 'Cotton Textiles and the Federal Child Labour Act of 1916', *Labour History* 16 (1975).

4 B. B. Gilbert, *British Social Policy, 1914–1939* (1970), 307.

5 Over unemployment insurance in 1931 and over bills to remove the defence of common employment in cases of injury to workers in 1933–5.

6 For an excellent discussion of this issue, see P. Hall, H. Land, R. Parker and A. Webb, *Change, Choice and Conflict in Social Policy* (1975), 157–230.

7 M. E. Rose, *The Relief of Poverty, 1834–1914* (1972).

8 Beveridge was a highly untypical and temporary civil servant at the time. J. F. Harris, *William Beveridge* (Oxford, 1977), appeared too late to be used, but it contains much evidence to test and criticize some of the ideas advanced in this Introduction.

I

Popular views and pressures for welfare

1 Sidney Webb: Evidence to the Royal Commission on Labour, 1892

Sidney Webb was a leading member of the Fabian Society and an acknowledged expert on social and labour issues. At this time he was a member of the London County Council for Deptford.

Collectivism is the economic obverse of democracy. . . . It appears to me that if you allow the tramway conductor to vote he will not forever be satisfied with exercising that vote over such matters as the appointment of the Ambassador to Paris, or even the position of the franchise. He will realize that the forces that keep him at work for sixteen hours a day for three shillings a day are not the forces of hostile kings, of nobles, of priests; but whatever forces they are he will, it seems to me, seek so far as possible to control them by his vote. That is to say, he will more and more seek to convert his political democracy into what one may roughly term an industrial democracy, so that he may obtain some kind of control as a voter over the conditions under which he lives.

> Royal Commission on Labour, *Minutes of Evidence, Fourth Report* (15 November 1892), 268

2 The view of the leadership of one trade union on the limitation of hours of work, 1888

In the 1880s and 1890s there was growing agitation for cutting the hours of labour. This document and the next illustrate the complexity of the issues involved, and the sophistication of working class responses to the idea of limiting hours and the means by which it should be achieved.

The real question to be decided is not whether we want an eight hours' working day, but whether it will be good policy to commence an agitation for it at the present time. We most unhesitatingly say it is not.

There is not an intelligent spinner in the four counties but what knows how, at the present time, our trade is being cramped by the protective policy of Continental and American nations. It is also no secret that in the Far East we have nothing to throw away. The men who are agitating for the eight hours a day have learned their creed from German agitators. Let the German and French and other continental workmen stick to their creed and reduce their own working hours to our level. Let us see about getting a real instead of a sham factory act for India. Let the workmen of industrial Europe and America, many of whom are fond of talking about the backwardness of British workmen in economical science, let them reach our standard, and then will be the time to consider whether we shall go on. Our remarks do not apply to the cotton industry alone. They apply to others with even greater force. Spinners have not a shred of foreign competition in our home markets. But there are scores of other trades that have. In ironwork, in boots and shoes, in cabinet work and harness, in lithographing; in fact, with the exception of cotton and coal, we are in almost every department of labour more or less subjected to foreign competition in our home markets. This competition comes from the very men who are at the bottom of this agitation for an eight hours' day.

Cotton Spinners' *Annual Report* (1888)

3 Engineering trade union members' views on the eight-hour day, 1891

Hull branch
I am requested by the members of this branch to send a rider to the schedule of the eight hours per day, or forty-eight per week, in relation to the third question.

It is as follows:
'That it is the opinion of the members of this branch that an eight-hours' day would be beneficial but the same to be obtained by our own exertions, believing it would be dangerous to trust our liberty in the hands of capitalists such as represent us in the present parliament.'

Leeds 5th branch
I am instructed to forward the following resolution, which was passed by this branch re the eight hours' question:
'That we, the members of the Leeds 5th branch desire to call the special attention of the executive council to the fact of the degradation we are enduring by the systematic organization of overtime, and earnestly ask the EC to use their power in first abolishing this, the greatest outrage on

our members. We should heartily welcome the fact of an eight hours' day, but would rather get the nine hours' day pure and simple, as we consider this by far the most important for the present.'

Birmingham 4th
This branch, by a large majority, refuses to fill up the schedule on this question, because, if the four questions are answered *seriatim* each member who voted would appear to regard the attainment of the eight hours' day as an immediately practicable question, and denounces the manner in which it has been submitted to the society as being likely to mislead. The following resolution and amendment were voted upon by the branch:
Resolution – 'This branch is of opinion that, bearing in mind the conditions of labour on the continent of Europe, where they work longer hours for less pay than ourselves, and also the general revival of protectionist principles over almost the whole of the civilized world, accompanied by the rise of tariffs hostile to our trade the present is quite the wrong time to take any steps towards attaining the eight hours' day.'
For, 27.

Amendment – 'This branch is of opinion that eight hours per day would be advantageous to us as a trade, and that it would be best to secure the same by act of parliament.'
For, 8.

Chatham branch
The following resolution was passed at our meeting:
'That we are of opinion that as it would be almost impossible to carry the eight hours per day until all the trades' unions are federated, we urge upon the local executive council to use their endeavours to forward the federation scheme with the ultimate end in view of the national federation of all classes of labour, whereby the workers could demand the eight hours' day without legislative aid.'
Carried.

> Amalgamated Society of Engineers (1891), branch returns on the question of the eight-hour day.

4   A friendly society perspective on social reform, 1894

The Foresters were one of the largest friendly societies. This extract reflects the views of those who proposed a collective working-class self-help as an alternative to individualism and to state welfare.

Thinking men will fail to see why capitalists should be relieved of their duty of contributing to the maintenance of many persons whose very poverty was caused by capitalists' appropriation of a very large measure of the fruits arising from the labour of those poor people who have to seek the aid of the rates in old age. . . . If a workman attends as diligently to his work as does his capitalist employer, why on earth should he not be made to rely on his wage to meet all his requirements as well as the employer depends upon his profits to meet all his requirements. . . . The aim of the working class ought to be to bring about economic conditions in which there should be no need for distribution of state alms. The establishment of a great scheme of state pensions would legalize and stamp as a permanent feature of our social life the chronic poverty of the age. The desire of the best reformers is to remove the conditions that make that poverty so that every citizen shall have a fair chance not only of earning a decent wage for today but such a wage as shall enable him to provide for the future. . . . Employers have presented carefully organized barriers to the workmen getting more wages. . . . We have always held that the only object of [reform] was to transfer the burdens from employer to labour. . . . Man is a responsible being. To rob him of his responsibility is to degrade him. The working class should rise to the occasion and insist upon being capable of using their own wages to their own advantage.

Foresters' Miscellany, leader (June 1894)

5 Trades unions, employers and old-age pensions, 1899

The National Committee of Organized Labour for Promoting Old-Age Pensions was set up by the trades unions and supported by some leading employers.

A conference upon the subject of old-age pensions was also suggested by Mr George Cadbury, and a special committee was formed, consisting of the officers and several members of the council, together with several members of friendly and cooperative societies. The conference was held on March 25th, in the hall of the technical school (kindly lent by the technical school committee). Five hundred and sixty-four delegates attended from various towns in the Midlands, representing some 350,000 members of trades councils, trades unions, friendly, cooperative, and other economic societies. Sixty-six members of city and town councils, school boards, and boards of guardians were present by invitation. An excellent address was delivered by Mr Charles Booth of London, who explained his suggestions for a universal system of old-age pensions, the principles being unanimously approved by the conference.

The success of the Birmingham conference (which was the last of seven held in various parts of the country) gave considerable impetus to the movement. The outcome of it is that a permanent local and national committee has been formed for the purpose of securing by legislation the adoption of a universal system of old-age pensions at sixty-five years of age.

The council expressed its appreciation of Mr George Cadbury's generosity in bearing the expense of the conference and nearly the whole of the expense of the town hall meeting.

The success of these two meetings depended much upon the action of members of the council, and it is not too much to say that had it not been for the existence of the trades council, in all probability they would not have been held.

> Birmingham Trades Council, *Annual Report*
> 33 (1899), 5

6   The reality of poverty, 1908–9

The following three documents give some indication of what it was like to be poor in Britain in the early years of this century.

I am A. Sailmaker to Trade but Sailing Ships being A. Thing of the past also sewing machines taking our place the Trade has left Me and having the misfortune to want the Leg. I go with A. Pinleg the trade suited me very well but I cannot get my living at it now upon an average I only work Three Months in A year the little I saved when Trade was good is done now. I do not now [*sic*] what to do unless I get employment that will suit my Case for I am Handicapped owing to the want of the Leg. I have been a Ratepayer for the last 28 years. I have A. wife and A. Daughter at School hoping you will give this your earnest Consideration an early reply or A. Personal interview will much oblige.

> Glasgow Distress Committee, Lord Provost's
> Fund (1908–9)

7   Mrs Hillon begs her sister-in-law to look after her children when she became disabled and had to go into Govan poorhouse, 1909

Dear Kate just a few lines to let you know that Mary and Jeanie is to be boarded away on Monday 8 and i did not know anything about it until

the last minute i expect patrack to go or to . . . patrack is fourteen is fit
to work mary and patrack say they will be very good and give you no
trouble if you will come and take them dear kate for the love of god try
and do something for the children for i know if they are with you they
will be all right the guvnor said when i got word from you i was to let
him know so you might right by return of post i hope you an maggie a
letty is very well so i have no more to say but i hope maggie is minding
her work so i hope and trust you will do something for the weans for
my hart is broke address Mrs Hill Govan combination hospital flats
ward 65 do this kate for mercy gods sake.

Glasgow City Archives, Govan Poor Relief
Records (8 February 1909)

8   Patrick MacGill: The life of a railway navvy, 1914

An evocation of life on the navvy gangs. Unlike the two previous documents
this account was written for publication.

Early on the morning of the next day, which was pay-day, Moleskin
was busy at work sounding the feelings of the party towards a great
scheme which he had in mind; and while waiting at the pay-office
when the day's work was completed, Joe made the following speech to
Red Billy's gang, all of whom, with the exception of Sandy
MacDonald, were present.

'Boys, Sandy MacDonald wants to go home and die in his own place',
said Joe, weltering into his subject at once. 'He'll kick the bucket soon,
for he has the look of the grave in his eyes. He only wants as much tin as
will take him home, and that is not much for any man to ask, is it? So
what do you say, boys, to a collection for him, a shillin' a man, or
whatever you can spare? Maybe some day, when you turn respectable,
one of you can say to himself, "I once kept myself from gettin' drunk,
by givin' some of my money to a man who needed it more than
myself." Now just look at him comin' across there.'

We looked in the direction of Joe's outstretched finger and saw
Sandy coming towards us, his rags fluttering around him like the duds
of a Michaelmas scarecrow.

'Isn't he a pitiful sight!' Moleskin went on. 'He looks like the Angel
of Death out on the prowl! It's a God's charity to help a man like Sandy
and make him happy as we are ourselves. We are at home here; he is
not. So it is up to us to help him out of the place. Boys, listen to me!'
Moleskin's voice sank into an intense whisper. 'If every damned man
of you don't pay a shillin' into this collection I'll look for the man that

doesn't, and I'll knuckle his ribs until he pays for booze for ev'ry man in Billy's shack, by God! I will.'

Everyone paid up decently, and on behalf of the gang I was asked to present the sum of three pounds fifteen shillings to Sandy MacDonald. Sandy began to cry like a baby when he got the money into his hands, and every man in the job called out involuntarily: 'Oh! you old fool, you!'

Pay-day was on Saturday. On Monday morning Sandy intended starting out on his journey home. All Saturday night he coughed out the long hours of the darkness, but in the morning he looked fit and well.   'You'll come through it, you fool!' said Moleskin. 'I'll be dead myself afore you.'

On the next night he went to bed early, and as we sat around the gaming table we did not hear the racking cough which had torn at the man's chest for months.

'He's getting better', we all said.

'Feeling all right, Sandy?' I asked, as I turned into bed.

'Mon! I'm feelin' fine now', he answered. 'I'm goin' to sleep well tonight, and I'll be fit for the journey in the morn.'

That night Sandy left us for good. When the morning came we found the poor wasted fellow lying dead in his bunk, his eyes wide open, his hands closed tightly, and the long finger-nails cutting into the flesh of the palm. The money which we gave to the man was bound up in a little leathern purse tied round his neck with a piece of string.

The man was very light and it was an easy job to carry him in the little black box and place him in his home below the red earth of Kinlochleven. The question as to what should be done with the money arose later. I suggested that it should be used in buying a little cross for Sandy's grave.

'If the dead man wants a cross he can have one', said Moleskin Joe. And because of what he said and because it was more to our liking, we put the money up as a stake on the gaming table. Clancy won the pile, because his luck was good on the night of the game.

That is our reason for calling him Clancy of the Cross ever since.

Patrick MacGill, *Children of the Dead End*
(1914), 239–42

9   A working class view of politics, 1911

This was one working-class reaction to the clauses in the Children Act of 1908 which prevented the giving of alcohol to children or taking them into public houses and also attempted to reduce cruelty to children.

As for giving a child a sip o' liquor, no doubt some people overdoes it, but I an't never see'd that chil'ern what had a drop o' what was going, be bigger drunkards than them what wasn't allowed to touch o' it; and publicans' chil'ern, what's always about in bars, don't turn out any worse than teetotallers' chil'ern. They kids us see'd to France, they took their wine, didn' 'em? Be they bigger drunkards over there than us be? 'Tis just the way to drive 'em into drink, to make a forbidden mystery o' it. Can tell they that makes these acts don' know chil'ern. Is that all o' it?

That's pretty well all that affects our sort, except the general clauses at the beginning about cruelty. . . . Cruelty! Aye! I s'pose if they heard the missis here say her'd knock the kids' heads off, they'd say her was a cruel mother, for all 'tis only a manner o' speaking, an' they there kids know it too. Chil'ern's Charter, do 'em call it? . . . Mischief-makers' opportunity, I say! Some o' it's all right, but half the time they that makes these laws don't know nort 't all 'bout it. Us bain't no crueller to our chil'ern on the whole than they be – a jolly sight easier wi' 'em in some ways, an' we has to hae 'em about 'long wi' us, kicking up their buzz, all the time, day an' night. They don't reckon what the likes o' us has to contend wi'; that'd be too much trouble; they flings laws and fines at our head instead. They don' know what 'tis for a woman, like missis here, to hae a houseful o' kids. 'Pretty little dears!' they says because 'tis chil'ern; and 'Poor little darlings!' if there's ort wrong; but you'd find that them as says it wouldn't look after 'em theirselves single-handed, an' do all the housework too, not for a day, n'eet for an hour nuther. Missis, her's got to let some o'it slide sometimes, an' 'tis a poor tally if her's got to suffer for what her can't help. Nine time out o' ten 'tis they as makes these laws what breaks 'em first, only they gets off by some means or other. I dearly loves chil'ern, an' I don't see why they shouldn't be kept a little bit thereafter, but all the same, I reckon that them as can afford nurses to look after 'em an' take 'em off their hands ought to have double punishment. That's never been thought of, I s'pose.

S. Reynolds, B. and T. Woolley, *Seems So*
(1911), 36–8

10 The Trades Union Congress: Social reform, 1907

We have for the time being settled our legal position and workmen's compensation. We urge our members to take up the following social and industrial reforms:

1 Miners' legal eight-hour day, and a reduction of hours in all trades
2 Old-age pensions
3 Unemployed
4 Compulsory state insurance
5 Land nationalization
6 Amendment of Poor Laws
7 Legal restriction of systematic overtime and
8 Housing of the working classes.

TUC, *Annual Report* (1907)

11 A syndicalist critique of labour exchanges and national insurance, 1913

Some groups on the left wing of the labour movement saw social reform as a step on the road to the Servile State, which Hilaire Belloc defined as 'That arrangement of society in which so considerable a number of families and individuals are constrained by positive law to labour for the advantage of other families and individuals as to stamp the whole community with the mark of such labour we call the Servile State.'

The credulity with which the forces of organized labour received the Insurance Act, especially Part II, must have caused just as much agreeable surprise to Mr Lloyd George and his army of capitalist camp-followers as it did resentment and misgiving amongst the advanced section of proletarian thinkers.

Wrapped in the cloven hoof of state paternalism could be clearly seen the insidious attempt of organized capital to tighten further the shackles of slavery around its exploited wage-slaves.

Add to this the following remarks of an ex-manager of a London labour exchange, and you have a system of espionage which cannot be outrivalled by Scotland Yard:

'Undoubtedly the workers are tricked under the auspices of the government. For instance, during my own connection with the labour exchange service, a cruel system was in vogue, which gives proof positive of the "People's" contention that the government encourage sweating. An applicant for work was asked whether he was a trade unionist or not. The question was put in quite a casual fashion – as though it were due merely to the inquirer's curiosity. Usually a man, even if he were suspicious, would rely on government protection against injustice, and answer. If he stated that he was a trade unionist then a private mark "T" would be placed upon his card. If on the other hand, he was a non-society worker, then "N" would be the record preserved at the exchange. Of course, the public explanation of such a dodge, if called for, would probably be that such a system ensures only non-union men being sent to masters who do not require unionists. But the real motive is to be found in the desire always to be prepared to collect the non-unionists together, and to provide strike-breakers in the event of unionists "downing tools".'

From the standpoint of the individual worker this system is venomous in the extreme. If a man is convicted of a crime against the civil law he enters the dock with the full knowledge that the bloodhounds of law and order have him safely gripped. But when he enters the labour exchange, having committed no other crime than that of being out of work, or a member of a union, or of bearing the characteristics of manly independence, how little he knows that he has sinned in the eyes of capitalist morality, and that he is condemned to a state of semi-starvation!

To make these institutions successful one thing was lacking, i.e., the power of coercion. All the while a worker could please himself whether he registered at the labour exchange, after a short experience he fought shy of them. But with the introduction of Part II of the Insurance Act those workers who come within its scope are forcibly embraced in its grip and subjected to its humiliating and degrading formalities.

Jack V. Wills, 'An Exposure of Labour Exchanges', *Solidarity* (September 1913), 5

12 Richard Roberts: old-age pensions, 1909

Roberts's mother kept a shop in Salford, Lancashire. Roberts's much praised account of his early life occasionally makes use of hindsight but does seem to reflect much of contemporary opinion on social reform.

Ever since the German *Reichstag* in 1889 had passed the model 'law of insurance against old age and infirmity' there had been much talk, but no action, in England about making similar provisions for the aged. At last, in 1908, the Liberal government allocated £1,200,000 for the establishment of a non-contributory old-age pension scheme and an act was passed to become law on 1 January 1909. Pensions, however, would be withheld from those 'who had failed to work habitually according to their ability and need, and those who had failed to save money regularly'. Here was a means test with a vengeance. Paupers were not entitled to any pension.

There was to be no doling out of largesse under the scheme.

Pensions were graduated from 1s to 5s a week, provided the recipients had already an income of less than £31 a year. The combined weekly allowance for a married couple was fixed at 7s 6d. Nevertheless, even these small doles meant life itself for many among the elderly poor. Old folk, my mother said, spending their allowance at the shop, 'would bless the name of Lloyd George as if he were a saint from heaven'. The government met with much opposition to the introduction of a pension scheme at all from both the middle and working classes. Free gifts of money, many urged, would dishearten the thrifty who saved for their old age, and encourage the idle. Lord Rosebery, the great Liberal peer, had even graver misgivings: the provision of old age pensions, he thought, 'might deal a blow at the Empire which could be almost mortal'. Meanwhile our elderly paupers still went to the workhouse.

R. Roberts, *The Classic Slum* (1973), 84

13   Basil Thompson: The seeds of revolution? 1918

Thompson was director of intelligence at the Home Office and his reports to the Cabinet on the activities of labour activists in the years after the first world war contributed to the mood of unease at the spread of revolutionary ideas in Britain.

During the past fortnight, the idea of direct action by the workers has certainly gained ground, especially in London. Among the advanced people there appears to be a quiet certainty that revolution is coming. One hears the remarks being made openly and with conviction and even among steady going socialists the wildest rumours are now beginning to circulate.

A private letter from Miss Sylvia Pankhurst to a friend in Glasgow, which has come into my hands, concludes with the words, 'I expect the revolution soon, don't you?'

Mr Will Thorne in conversation said a few days ago that Bolshevism, or rather the state of dissatisfaction that might foster it, has never been so high in England as at the present moment. The industrial workers of Scotland are of a deeper red than the usual red-flaggers. There is growing unrest among the railway workers, which will soon make itself felt. He went on to say that there would be no revolution in England, not in his lifetime, but that it would come on the Continent.

Miss Sylvia Pankhurst, who has just completed a week's tour of propaganda in Glasgow, said that in Scotland there were 'patches' where the Industrial Workers of the World were of some numerical strength. She also stated that the Silver Badge men are the most attentive of her audience, and that the 'Dreadnought', especially in Sheffield, was eagerly bought up by them. She admitted, however, that the working man's interest in Bolshevism was flagging, and that they were more intent on the doings of the German Socialists than on what was going on in Russia. In the smaller towns and villages of Scotland she found that what interested the people were pensions, the cost of living, unemployment, the return of the soldiers in time for Christmas, and the land question.

> PRO Cab 24/71, Fortnightly Report on revolutionary organizations in the United Kingdom and Morale Abroad (2 December 1918)

14   The Trades Union Congress: Family allowances, 1930

The TUC found it difficult to support family allowances in the 1930s, fearing that such allowances would lead to the neglect of other social services or would interfere with wage negotiations.

Minority report of joint committee on family allowances adopted by the general council

1   We regret that we are unable to concur in the recommendations made by the majority of our colleagues on the committee, and we therefore submit this minority report.

2   We agree entirely that further financial provision is urgently needed for the improvement of the health, education and general well-being of the children. We differ only in our view as to the most effective and economical means to that end in the present circumstances of the nation.

3   We wish to record our conviction at the outset that working-class mothers would spend cash allowances with the utmost economy and with unselfish regard for their children. We do not differ from our colleagues on this point, and our case does not rest on any belief that cash allowances would be squandered or diverted to wrong channels. Such a belief, if held by anyone, is in our view utterly false and may be disregarded in any discussion of the question.

4   Nor do we wish to argue at length the question of the possible effects which a system of cash payments might have upon wage negotiations and collective agreements, though we are quite satisfied that such a system would affect detrimentally negotiations regarding

wage fixing. We do feel, however, that if any comparison with social services is to be made on this point, the cash allowance system is more likely to affect the unions adversely. Beyond expressing this opinion we do not go into the question at all.

5   We must further make it clear that we do not oppose the system of cash payments because of any fundamental objection to the principle of cash as against services.

6   Despite the protestations of the majority of the committee regarding the desirability of further extending the social services, we are forced to the conclusion that at the present time the payment of cash allowances would have to be an alternative to further developments of social services. . . .

9   We believe, in short, that the development of the national health, education and other social services is so vital in the interests of the workers' children that all the funds available for such social purposes should be spent in extending these services, until they are completed, rather than in paying out cash allowances.

10   We *therefore recommend* that before any decision on family allowances is taken, the following social services should be fully established out of public funds:

 (i) A complete medical service (preventive and treatment) for all children from birth to the school-leaving age.
 (ii) Pre-natal and post-natal maternity service, together with a cash payment for each child for the first year or two years after birth.
(iii) The raising of the school-leaving age, with adequate maintenances allowance during the additional year.
(iv) The provision of nursery schools for children up to the age of admission to elementary schools.
 (v) The provision of adequate healthy houses.
(vi) The elimination of tuberculosis and the provision of pure milk.

Trades Union Congress, *Annual Report* (1930),
218–19

15   The hunger marches of the 1930s

The National Unemployed Workers Movement organized a series of marches and demonstrations throughout Britain in protest against unemployment, cuts in social benefits and the means test. This is part of an account of one of these marches by Harry McShane, one of the leaders of the NUWM.

Our demands
   1   Abolition of the means test.

2   That children of unemployed be granted 1s 6d per week extra, and that adult unemployed and adult dependants be granted 3s per week extra. These increases to apply to all unemployed whether in receipt of statutory or transitional payments or in receipt of public assistance.

3   That rents be reduced 25 per cent.

4   That relief work be provided at TU wages and conditions.

5   That the social service schemes and all voluntary labour connected with same be repudiated. In addition, the lifting of the embargo on the Soviet Union and conclusion of a new trade agreement.

The hunger march of June 1933 was a coping stone to a whole series of mass activities which had swept Scotland. In Glasgow, in Renfrewshire, in Fifeshire, Lanarkshire, Dunbartonshire, even in far north Aberdeen and Fraseburgh, the mass movement of the unemployed had developed. Despite sneers, insults, batonings, jailings the agitation had developed, thousands of meetings held, incessant delegations and deputizing, huge popular petitions containing the demands of the unemployed organized, mass demonstrations held. Clashes with the police were frequent (in Glasgow, due to plain clothes policemen provocation, a fierce fight took place on Glasgow Green and fourteen policemen were injured). A tremendous petition, containing the signatures of over 112,000 people was organized, a concession of 1s 6d per child literally torn out of the Glasgow PAC by mass pressure – only to have the National Government step in, in order to prevent a workers' victory in Glasgow.

In Fife, in Dumbartonshire, even in Ayrshire, the workers forced concessions.

County hunger marches in Fife, Ayrshire, Lanarkshire, were organized. They were very successful. More and more workers were being brought into the struggle; hope was being given to the fainthearted and the lukewarm. The struggle against the means test, the dole cuts, the Anomalies Act was intensifying. The stage was set for an all-Scottish hunger march to raise the fight to a still greater height. The famous hunger march in June was the result.

Not an isolated event, not a stunt, but the logical development, the coping stone, of the mass local activities throughout the winter and spring.

H. McShane, *Three Days that Shook Edinburgh: Story of the Historic Scottish Hunger March* (1933)

16   The Trades Union Congress: The Beveridge Report, 1942

TUC initiative had led to the setting up of the Interdepartmental Committee on Social Services. Their detailed plans should be compared with those being put forward by employers and with those of the Beveridge Report itself.

The general council, therefore, as a result of their detailed consideration, submit that the following should be the governing principles for reconstruction of social insurance and allied services:

1   Cash benefit in respect of industrial accidents and industrial diseases should be dealt with and administered under separate and specific workmen's compensation legislation.

2   There should be an inclusive scheme to cover unemployment, sickness, maternity, non-compensatable accidents, invalidity, old age, blindness, death and widowhood and orphanhood. The scheme should cover all gainfully occupied persons irrespective of income as defined in the Personal Injuries (Civilians) Scheme, viz. 'a person who is engaged in any trade, business, profession, office, employment or vocation and is wholly or substantially dependent thereon for a livelihood, or a person, who though temporarily unemployed, is normally so engaged and dependent'.

3   There should be a flat rate of benefit which for a commencement should be £2 per week plus dependants' allowances, this to be the amount payable to adults in respect of unemployment, sickness, maternity, invalidity, non-compensatable accidents, widowhood, blindness and old age.

Unemployment benefit should be implemented with a scheme for transfer allowances (lodging, removal, etc.) to make it possible for people to move when their industry has closed down.

Widowhood   A young widow of working age with no children should not continue to receive benefit if she finds employment but should inherit her husband's insurance rights under the scheme and have equal employment opportunities with men.

Old-age pensions should begin at 65 for men and 60 for women as at present and the pension should only be paid on retirement from work at the determined age. If a pensioner returns to work he should forfeit the pension whilst working.

Maternity   The cash benefit of £2 per week should be paid for the maternity period, subject to any scheme which may be worked out.

Death   The amount in view is £20 on the death of the insured person.

Orphanhood   The figure in mind is 15*s* per week up to the age of 16 or as long as the child remains at school. Benefit should continue during the whole period of the contingency provided against.

Persons not entitled to benefit should be provided for by a body like the present assistance board, properly constituted and remodelled to meet the situation and operating on a personal means test. This would involve the abolition of local authority public assistance committees.

4   There should be a flat rate of contribution and the proportion might be 25 per cent from insured persons, 25 per cent from employers and 50 per cent from the state. Contributions should only be payable in respect of the present contribution schemes including death benefit. This proposal would ensure that contributions would not be paid for benefits not now on a contributory basis, e.g. blindness.

5   The scheme should come under the direction of one ministry with special arrangements for health services.

6   A comprehensive national medical service covering everything that medical science can command for prevention and cure of sickness should be provided by the nation and be made available to everybody in the state. This service should include a statistical department for the provision of occupational and geographical records necessary to safeguard the health of the people. There should also be associated with the medical services a complete rehabilitation service on up-to-date lines.

7   The council appreciate that the principles recommended affect the activities of approved societies in addition to services now financed and controlled by national or municipal authorities. Any system of complete coordination of such services involves either the abolition of approved societies, in their present form, or handing over to such societies services now under national or municipal control. The whole aim and purpose of social service is completely inconsistent with the furtherance of commercial interests and there should be no room for that in the new scheme. Bodies like trade unions, however, with their long and honourable tradition of service ought to be preserved so that the benefit of their experience and goodwill can be utilized in administration on behalf of the state. Local authorities should be regarded as the medium for translating into action national policy in their localities for such services as may be decided.

8   The general council urge that in the consideration of any coordinating scheme of social service adequate provision should be

made to safeguard the interests of persons employed in all the existing schemes.

Memorandum by the Trades Union
Congress, Social Insurance and Allied
Services, Cmd. 6405 (1942), 16–17

17   Communist criticism of social reform as proposed by employers, 1942

Though the Beveridge Report was widely welcomed by the labour movement, some groups on the left were suspicious of alternative proposals for social reform emanating from employers at the same time. The details of the proposals attacked here are in document 33.

Last summer General Ritchie saw what he thought was a promising gap in Rommel's defences and dashed at it with the bulk of his armoured forces. Alas! it was a carefully baited trap and the British army sustained a heavy defeat.

The trade unions of Britain are now being invited by 120 leading industrialists in a statement on 'A National Policy for Industry' to walk into a similar trap.

The 120 signatories are prominent on the boards of leading large-scale business enterprises, ranging from the Imperial Chemical Industries which recognizes the trade unions, through J. and P. Coats, the great cotton thread combine, the bulk of whose employees are unorganized, to Ford Motors, who refuse to recognize any trade unions whatsoever.

Their bait for the unions is the advocacy of a 'code of obligations towards employees' as a first charge on industry. . . .

In fact the industrialists propose to surrender to the workers social territory from which they could not very well exclude them anyhow. . . .

In return for this concession of what they cannot withhold, the employers hope to trap the unions into supporting the organization of all industry in a series of powerful monopolies which will be linked together in a central council for industry.

Naturally, the industrialists disclaim any selfish intention to restrict output and keep up prices in the interests of the powerful groups who will control these monopolies. They want 'the lowest possible price consistent with the adequate remuneration of labour and capital', which is a monopolist's stock formula.

But they strongly object to 'uneconomic investment and production', insist on the 'discouragement of wasteful and destructive competition', and declare that state compulsion may be necessary to force recalcitrant firms into the proposed industrial monopolies.

They admit, however, that 'trade associations can be operated merely for price maintenance, incidentally affording protection to the inefficient or high-cost producer rather than for the general good,' and do not give one good reason why their new 'sectional associations' (as they call their proposed industrial monopolies) will not act precisely in this way. . . .

The bait is, however, not too unattractive from the trade union point of view.

After all, the government has subsidized certain industries, and permitted others to increase prices, in order to enable wages to be raised. Why should not the unions cooperate with the employers in particular industries to get as much as possible from the common pool? The more they get, some short-sighted people will argue, the higher wages they will be able to pay.

A dangerous trap and one destructive of working-class solidarity. A single monopoly in a sea of unorganized industries may make special gains at the expense of the rest and dole out a few extra crumbs to its employees. But if every industry tries to operate a policy of monopoly and restriction of output, the only result is high prices, stubborn mass unemployment, the undermining of trade unionism, the drive for foreign markets and war.

To accept such a policy is to disrupt the labour movement, for illusory sectional advantages.

J. R. Campbell, *Daily Worker* (25 November 1942), from C. Madge, *Industry After the War* (1943), 53

II

Employers and welfare: efficiency and social control

18   Birmingham Chamber of Commerce: Labour exchanges, 1905

Birmingham Chamber of Commerce was among the earliest advocates of a national system of labour exchanges to serve the needs of industry and to provide information necessary before the problem of unemployment could be tackled. The exchanges were to be kept entirely separate from the Poor Law.

Before any really practical attempt can be made to prepare a national scheme – and only a national scheme can be deemed satisfactory – for dealing with the unemployed on sound lines, it is essential that permanent machinery be constructed for obtaining reliable information as to the number of persons out of work who are entitled to be classed as bona fide unemployed, that is to say, men who, through some cause over which they have no control, are temporarily out of work – men who will work when they have it to do. These men are assets of the nation, and it devolves on the nation to see that they are not allowed to become pauperized. With regard to the other class, the unemployable, the wastrel and the loafer, the sternest measures are necessary. Life has too long been made easy for this class, who thrive most when unemployment is greatest. It is desirable that they should be sifted out and then it would not be difficult to adopt measures for dealing with them.

We believe that the only possible way of obtaining the information which is necessary is to inaugurate a permanent system of labour registries under the control of the Board of Trade, and the bodies which naturally suggest themselves for this kind of work are the chambers of commerce.

Birmingham Chamber of Commerce Journal (1905)

19   W. H. Lever (Lord Leverhulme): Welfare and efficiency, 1906–17

These extracts from Lever's speeches between 1906 and 1917 show his insistence on the connection between welfare and business efficiency and the need for state intervention to ensure that all employers provide the same standards for their labour forces.

There could be no worse friend to labour that the benevolent, philanthropic employer who carries his business on in a loose, lax manner, showing 'kindness' to his employees; because, as certain as that man exists, because of his looseness and laxness, and because of his so-called kindness, benevolence, and lack of business principles, sooner or later he will be compelled to close. On the other hand, although it sounds hard, that man who adheres strictly to business principles, who pays, of course, the highest rate of wages, because today it is not possible to pay less, and carries on his business on so-called 'hard' lines, will not be the worst friend of labour at all. This man who is employing labour on strictly business principles is not the least respected by labour in any way, and ought not to be.

If the nineteenth century was responsible for the triumphant introduction of new methods for the creation of wealth, the twentieth century must see the triumph of the introduction of new methods of the more equal distribution of wealth. But in realizing, or attempting to realize, the better distribution of wealth, we must not fall behind in our power or efficiency to produce wealth. Therefore, modern developments must progress along the well-defined lines of efficiency.

I think the first fact that we must recognize is that, in the coming days, the employer will not be considered to be the sole arbiter of the conditions of employment, nor will the employee. The time is coming – and coming very rapidly – when both employer and employee must be more subject than they are today to control by the state. It is not merely a question of the rights and duties of employer and employee, but we know now that the public, the consumer, and, in fact, the well-being of the state and of the Empire have also to be considered. We have not yet developed to the point that we can be trusted, any of us, to be unselfish from the highest motives of enlightened self-interest. The education and health and training in efficiency of the whole nation depend upon the hours of labour and the conditions of employment.

I know that there is a preconceived false idea in many minds that welfare work in factories is largely a question of canteens, model villages, free libraries, and so on; but, in my opinion, welfare work in factories is much more a question of wages and hours, of ventilation in the factory, of cubical air space, of heating and lighting and sanitation, than it is a question of any of the so-called welfare work of canteens and so on. Every fact, circumstance, and condition of employment affecting the workers engaged in a factory or office – mentally, physically, or materially – must come within its scope.

W. H. Lever, *The Six-Hour Day* (1917)

20   An employer argues for compulsory insurance, 1907

John Macaulay was the general manager of the Alexandra (Newport and South Wales) Docks. He gave evidence to the Royal Commission on the Poor Laws of 1905–9, in which he argued for compulsory insurance against sickness and old age and for strict control of the 'criminal and defective classes'.

The present system of workhouses and casual wards for the destitute is one which induces the loss of self-respect. Moreover, the assistance so rendered is, in the majority of cases, too late to be of any benefit to the recipient. Some such system as that known as the 'Elberfeld' system in Germany should be adopted, in which the great point is to keep the poor from becoming destitute. Care of the unfortunate and poor should be the direct duty of individual citizens. The encouragement afforded to the vagrant population of the country by the creation of casual wards should be abandoned, and, as in the Elberfeld system, it should be made more difficult for tramps and other suspicious persons to become burdensome to a community to which they are strangers.

A great deal could also be done to lessen the effect of occasional unemployment by making insurance against sickness and old age compulsory to the extent of a definite percentage of a man's or woman's earnings. For this purpose the many friendly societies might with advantage be amalgamated and placed under the control of the state. All forms of sweating labour should be abolished, as well as the employment of child labour. The legal obligation of supporting relations in distress might also be more strictly enforced.

Laboratories for the study of criminal paupers and the defective classes should be created, presided over by men of the highest intellectual attainments in order to investigate and elucidate and suggest remedies for the many forms of physical and mental degeneration which affect the labouring classes.

Some such system as the 'Borstal' might with advantage be introduced for dealing with 'young-adult' criminals and first offenders, and lastly emigration might be largely encouraged, and, if need be, more liberally state-aided.

In conclusion I would like to add that as the result of the many years' experience I have had, during which I have been thrown into contact with individuals belonging to many varied classes of labour, and during which I have witnessed many failures through one or another of the causes I have mentioned, it is my firm conviction that anything like permanent benfit to the workers can be obtained, not by the introduction of machinery for dealing in an arbitrary method with individual cases, but by an investigation of the root causes underlying the distress of sections of the working classes as a whole, and by the application of remedies which will transform the evil conditions which are the bases of the troubles sought to be cured.

> Royal Commission on the Poor Laws, *Minutes of Evidence* (1907)

21   Birmingham Chamber of Commerce: Bismarckian social insurance, 1907

Birmingham Chamber of Commerce continued its campaign for a comprehensive social insurance scheme on Bismarckian lines and argued the case before the Association of Chambers of Commerce. A resolution on similar lines was accepted by the Association at its next meeting and pressed on the Liberal government.

National insurance against accident, sickness, etc.
Mr J. S. Taylor (Birmingham) moved:

'That this association is of opinion that the time has arrived when His Majesty's Government should take into serious consideration the subject of national insurance for the working classes against accident, sickness, invalidity, and old age on the lines, so far as is practicable, of the comprehensive system which has operated so successfully in Germany; and that a memorial be presented to the prime minister and the home secretary praying that they will be pleased to receive a deputation from this association to urge upon them the desirability of a royal commission being appointed to inquire into and report upon the subject.'

In doing so, he said the resolution related to a question of serious moment to taxpayers – a question upon the proper solution of which the future industrial efficiency of this country largely depended. The resolution related to a problem which had to be faced by the country, and that if they did not face it voluntarily they would sooner or later be compelled to face it by the sheer march of events. The Labour Party, which had, by undaunted effort, secured a prominent place in the councils of the nation, had decided views upon the question – views with which most of those present would find themselves not in accord – and if commercial men, through apathy or ignorance, pursued a policy of drift, then there was a likelihood that the specious arguments of the Labour Party would secure the adoption by the country of their views, and the commercial classes, who were nevertheless vitally concerned, would have to submit to them.

The characteristics of the British race had always been independence and self-reliance, and out of those characteristics sprang trade unions with their sick and out-of-work and old-age benefit funds; sick societies, friendly societies, savings banks, and similar institutions, by means of which the thrifty working man had been enabled, at small expense, to make provision against some of the more distressing contingencies of life. It was the spirit which had fostered this kind of thing which ought to be developed, because it was thrift of that character which conduced to independence and self-reliance. Legislation which led to a slackening of personal responsibility could only be pernicious in its results; whilst legislation which tended to strengthen the feeling of personal responsibility must be pre-eminently beneficial, not only to the individual, but to the state.

It was almost certain that the financial cost of the English system represented a heavier burden on employers of labour and on the community than the German system of threefold state insurance. He thought enough had been said to prove that the German system of national insurance was deserving of serious consideration by the English government. It was already admitted that something must be done for the further protection of the industrial classes against the contingencies and uncertainties of their existence, and no scheme had yet been suggested in parliament or out which was equal in any way to the German system.

Association of Chambers of Commerce of the
United Kingdom, Annual Report (1907)

22   A deputation of shipbuilding and engineering employers to the Board of Trade on labour exchanges in 1909

Frederick Henderson, a Glasgow shipbuilder, puts the case for amalgamating workmen's compensation legislation and national unemployment insurance, with the workers contributing to both. Churchill, the President of the Board of Trade, in reply accepts this point and stresses the extent to which the workers have been persuaded to accept novelty and agrees on the need to prevent malingering.

Mr Henderson: There was one thing I said in a joke, but I do want to say it in earnest now; you are going to begin your Unemployment Insurance Bill, and I think you should consider the question of coordinating the Workmen's Compensation Act, and insist that the workmen pay one third, the employer pays one third, and the government pays one third, because the Unemployment Insurance Bill will be a very much more costly bill, and it would be a much fairer bill to the employers if you thought seriously of doing that. I put that suggestion forward with all humility. We are suffering now seriously and are meeting more stringent competition every year, and if anything can be done to minimize our burden it would be doing good to the workmen, because our interests are identical. If you were to do that, it would prevent malingering. At the present moment when we go to court we know that there are cases of negligence, but it is one thing to prove it, and another to know it. Over and over again we take cases to the court, and they get the cheap sympathy of the sheriff or the local judge, and compensation is given to the poor working man. We know of cases over and over again where men who do not deserve a farthing get handsome compensation because we cannot bring it home.

Sir H. Llewellyn Smith: The unemployment insurance we propose to keep out of the courts.

The president: I have no doubt that ultimately you will have these things consolidated – old-age pensions, accidents, infirmity, invalidity, and so on, they will all be rolled into one, and all be on a contributory basis. I have no doubt in the future it will come to that. Mind you, these contributory insurances are quite a new step, the workmen have never been ready to do it before; we have never been able to get them so far as that before. There is a good deal going on now which you do not feel wholeheartedly in sympathy with, but you ought to watch this one point, that all future developments of the old-age pension schemes are going to be on a contributory basis, and not a non-contributory basis. That is clear; and the employing classes in this country have at any rate the fact before their eyes that the door is closed to the handing out of doles on a great scale. I am quite prepared to defend the Old-Age Pensions Act, that is another point, but my point is that the extension which you were afraid of, which looked as if it was inevitable, that it should go down to 65 and take another 15 millions, and that one party should bid against the other with a view to winning elections year by year – that is at a finish, because we are going on a contributory scheme now in which the workman will pay, and in which he will have an interest in seeing that there is no fraud.

Mr Henderson: There ought to have been a contributory system with regard to the workmen's compensation. Then there would have been no malingering, or it would have been very much minimized.

The president: I quite agree.

PRO Lab 2/211/LE 500 (1909). Deputation of Engineering and Shipbuilding Employers (18 August 1909)

23   Sir Benjamin C. Browne, 1909

Sir Benjamin Browne was one of the most influential employers of his day. He was chairman of Hawthorne, Leslie and Co. Ltd, shipbuilders and engineers at Newcastle-on-Tyne and leading figure in the Engineering Employers Federation. Here he is consulted by Sir Hubert Llewellyn Smith, permanent secretary of the Board of Trade about the Board's proposals for unemployment insurance in the early preparatory stages.

(Confidential)

St Peter's Works
Newcastle-on-Tyne
22nd February 1909

Dear Sir Hubert

I went carefully through the memorandum you gave me on Friday afternoon, and have been thinking about it ever since.

The first thing that strikes me, I fear, you will think of rather a revolutionary character. Do you not think it would be better to leave out of your scheme altogether the mechanic, or, say, to make the scheme only apply to men of 30s a week and under? I observe that, especially in shipyards, mechanics not only are perfectly able to provide for moderate times of unemployment, but very often appear to like them.

The mechanic is, I think, altogether too well off to need the support of either government or of his employer. Of course, if there comes a period when he is off work for a year or two, it is wholly different, but your proposals are not, as I understand, calculated to deal with such cases as this.

But when from the skilled mechanic we turn to the ordinary labourer who has, say, £1 a week and a family, the case is wholly different, and I believe the value of your scheme would be very great indeed. As a class, he would never be willingly out of work; if he has children he really cannot save, and his employment is at all times much more precarious than that of the mechanic, and I think, to him, the scheme would be a real boon, and if you make a wage limit above which it did not act, we might hope that, as years went on, the ordinary process of raising wages would draw more and more men out of the scheme, so that it would always apply only to those who are liable to be in real distress even by temporary cessations of work.

> Beveridge Papers III 37/A/4 6–8
> (22 February 1909)

24 Sydney Buxton, 1911

Buxton succeeded Churchill as president of the Board of Trade. Here he tries to meet a common objection that contributions to an unemployment insurance scheme will tend to increase unemployment. In doing so he makes the connection between welfare and efficiency.

Employer objections

Some employers have said that their contributions will either be transferred to the consumer or be deducted from the workmen's wages. What is your answer to this suggestion?

It may of course happen that the contribution of the employers will ultimately fall on the consumer, but what employers ought to remember is that this is no additional burden on the country or necessarily on any particular trade. The burden of unemployment is already met in various ways. It is only really rearranged in, as we believe, a way which will be much less uncomfortably borne and it will, we hope, in the end diminish unemployment and therefore the burden. The employer's contribution must no doubt be distributed. Its economic gravitation will make it settle somehow, but it will be less of a burden and more easily borne. Moreover we hope that the expenditure will be fruitful in so improving the physique and morale of labour as to prevent any rise eventually in cost. That is a matter for the future, but if the scheme is successful it ought to pay as a business proposition.

> *Morning Post* (12 May 1911)

25 Sir Charles W. Macara: Campaign against the National Insurance Bill, 1911

Macara was another influential employer of the period and unofficial spokesman of the Lancashire cotton industry. He preferred conciliation and collective bargaining to social welfare through the state and he founded the Employers' Parliamentary Association to fight the National Insurance Act. His campaign failed but the organization survived to become part of the Federation of British Industries in 1917.

Apart from the campaign I led in opposition to Mr Joseph Chamberlain and his tariff reform scheme, no other crusade in which I was concerned was so fiercely fought as that in which I was engaged when the Right Hon. D. Lloyd George introduced his German scheme of national health insurance.

I entered into the keenest opposition to the bill from the very start, as I saw in it nothing but a sheer waste of our resources, while it was clear to all but those blinded by political prejudice that its incidence would be a heavy tax upon industry and would work most inequitably as between one trade and another.

Primarily, of course, I was concerned for my own industry of cotton, where I could see that employers would be penalized to an extent far beyond what was just, and altogether out of proportion to other trades which required much less manual help to carry on their business. An industry the wages in which represented 50 per cent of the cost of production would obviously be unduly handicapped in comparison with other industries where much less labour was employed in proportion to the capital invested, while coal, upon which the cotton trade depended so largely, would be in an even worse position than cotton. The wages in the coal industry at that time were fully 70 per cent of the cost of production. Now the position in the industry is even worse, for wages have reached quite 80 per cent of the total cost.

Sir Charles W. Macara, *Recollections* (1921), 217

26   Lanarkshire coal owners: The National Insurance Act, 1911

This extract indicates one response to the National Health Insurance Act. Other employers wound up their own private or contributory benefit schemes.

No money benefits will be paid under the National Insurance Act of 1911 for six months after 15.7.1911, so medical fees will be deducted from workmen for that period by arrangement with the Miners Federation. As the act does not provide medical attendance for the wives and families of insured workmen a conference was held with the doctors and representatives of the Miners Federation whereby wives and families would be medically attended, by workmen paying a flat rate of $1\frac{1}{2}$ pence per week without medicine or 2 pence with medicine. These rates are being deducted at most collieries.

> Lanarkshire Coal Masters Association, Annual Report of Executive Committee, Scottish Record Office, CB.8.2 (24 March 1913)

27   Seebohm Rowntree: Welfare in wartime, 1917

The first world war reinforced concern among employers about the connections between welfare and efficiency and social control. Rowntree, whose pioneering social survey of York had done much to mould pre-war opinion, was brought in to advise Lloyd George on welfare in munitions factories. The extracts are from an address circulated to employers and welfare supervisors.

I think we may define welfare work as the provision of an environment which will enable everyone to be and to do his best. We are here primarily concerned with industrial welfare, but our conception of this, and the organization we adopt in order to secure it, will be on the wrong lines if we attempt to isolate it from the well-being of the community as a whole. Rather, in all our efforts to promote it we should recognize the fact that we cannot separate a man's life as a citizen from his life as a worker. If you would have a permanently efficient worker you must have a good citizen, adequately paid, and well-developed in body and in mind, with a healthy outlook on the world, with keen and worthy ambition, and a true conception of his responsibilities to his fellow workers, to the firm for which he works and to the community. Whatever tends to create or to develop these qualities is in the true sense welfare work.

As for what we are especially concerned with here, welfare work in industry, it is nothing new, though recently, for many reasons, it has become increasingly self-conscious. It has existed as long as industry itself has existed.

First of all the factors in welfare, I should put the payment of adequate wages, because without it we really have no firm foundation on which to build up other ideal conditions. The present scale of wages is, in my opinion, entirely inadequate, so far as unskilled labour is concerned. I think we must look forward to a very much higher standard of wages in this country for unskilled workers, and doubtless the standard for skilled workers will rise also, though not, I think, in a proportionate degree. I would put the wage at which we should immediately aim at making an absolute minimum at about 35s a week at pre-war prices, and a very great deal more than that now.

Now, in order to pay those increased wages, we must have greatly increased productivity, for two reasons. The first is that without it, industry, as at present constituted, could not afford such wages.

But to secure men against unemployment is real sound welfare work, because a sense of chronic insecurity is definitely opposed to social well-being, as well as to industrial productivity. A man cannot build up a healthy, vigorous working life if he never knows from day to day whether his income is going to cease.

I come to the point in which the services of the welfare workers are most essential, namely in improving the relationship between capital and labour. A great deal of our low productivity at the present time is due to the fact that, instead of getting on with the job, we are more or less consciously in a state of hostility and tension. We are supicious of our workers, our workers are supicious of us, and when we should be putting all our strength and thought into our business, and increasing output to the utmost limit, we are frittering away our energies in contradicting, and abusing and hampering one another. We must change all this if we are to get high productivity.

> A. Briggs, *Social Thought and Social Action: A Study of the Work of Seebohm Rowntree, 1871–1954* (1961)

28   National Industrial Conference, 1919

Called at the height of the post-war industrial unrest, the National Industrial Conference marked the high point in employers' support for welfare. The proposals for extending unemployment insurance, stabilizing employment and house building did not meet with unanimous support among employers and were later withdrawn.

Sub-committee – unemployed

Memorandum submitted by employers' representatives on 18th March 1919

Maintenance of the unemployed

1   Employers are in favour of making provision for unemployment by extending and adapting the scheme of insurance embodied in the National Insurance Act, 1911, Part II.

2   Employers are of the opinion that such provisions should not be confined to employees engaged in certain trades as at present but should be extended to employees in all trades with certain exceptions.

The employers are of the view, however, that unemployment benefit should be on a more reasonable scale than that provided for in the act of 1911.

With regard to the union's memorandum of 17th March 1919, the employers have the following observations to make:

Under-consumption   Increased wealth is necessary to a higher standard of life and this can only be obtained by increased production.

Increased output and higher wages are necessary to the prosperity of employers and employed and unless efficient work goes with higher wages the result will be disastrous to both the employers and employed, and increased output must be maintained if higher wages are to be uniformly paid. By increasing the output the cost of manufacture per unit would decrease and the employers would be placed in a position to successfully compete and at the same time employ a greater number of workpeople. The spending power of the greater number of workpeople employed would correspondingly increase with a cheaper production of commodities. A large consumption of commodities would make greater production necessary and consequently a greater number of workpeople would be employed.

Stabilizing employment   As far as practicable, public work should be reserved for periods of slackness. The employers suggest as regards such work the government or municipalities should as far as possible anticipate periods of slackness in order that they may be in a position to place orders immediately a period of slackness commences rather than after the slackness has been in operation for some time.

State development of industry   The employers agree that there is urgent necessity for a comprehensive housing scheme throughout the country.

> National Industrial Conference, Subcommittee 3, unemployment, Department of Employment Library, GP 331.1 (18 March 1919)

29   Birmingham Chamber of Commerce: Labour exchanges, 1920

By 1920 even Birmingham Chamber of Commerce was coming to doubt the value of the system of labour exchanges, which they had strongly urged on government only fifteen years before. Employers' attitudes to welfare were not static or unchanging, but were related to the perceived needs of business and the success or failure of welfare in meeting these changing needs.

Birmingham business men and labour exchanges

Soon after the appointment by the minister of labour of the committee to examine and report upon the working and administration of labour exchanges, the Birmingham Chamber of Commerce issued to its members a questionnaire. To this 1,112 replies were received, and upon these it was decided to present oral evidence. The following is a copy of the witnesses' proof which was sent to the committee:

A short time ago a questionnaire was addressed to the members of the chamber and up to the time of preparing this proof 1,112 replies had been received, which are summarized in the following paragraphs:

(a) When in need of workpeople has it been either invariably or occasionally your practice to apply to the labour exchange?

In answer to this the following replies were received:

170 firms stated that they invariably applied to the labour exchange.

110 firms stated that they did not so apply.

715 firms stated that they occasionally applied.

54 firms stated that they had at one time applied.

(b) Have your requests been promptly responded to?

In answer to this, the following replies were received:

479 firms in the affirmative.

239 firms in the negative.

221 firms say that occasionally the requests have been promptly responded to.

(c) Have the workpeople sent to you been suitable and in accordance with your requirements as to trade or skill?

In answer to this question the following replies were received:

27 firms in the affirmative.

769 firms in the negative.

143 firms replied that occasionally the workpeople sent were suitable.

(d) In your opinion do the labour exchanges supply a substantial need or have you a simpler or better method of obtaining workpeople?

In answer to this question the following replies were received:

606 firms replied that the labour exchanges did not supply a substantial need.

333 firms replied that advertisements in the press were more productive.

(e) Are the labour exchanges worth the large amount of national money which is expended on their buildings and administration?

In answer to this question the following replies were received:
1,010 firms replied to the effect that labour exchanges were not worth the money expended upon them.

I would add that, generally speaking, when labour exchanges have been mentioned at meetings of the chamber and the council and its committees, the views expressed have invariably been against the continuance of the system, on the ground that it has failed to supply any real need.

With the increasing organization of workers into trade unions the need for labour exchanges is less than ever, and the manufacturers are not impressed by figures as to the number of vacancies filled, especially as they have no information as to the period during which men employed through the labour exchanges continue in the employment to which they are sent, and for which they are engaged.

Birmingham Chamber of Commerce Journal (1920)

30   The Royal Commission on National Health Insurance: The costs of social welfare, 1926

These extracts from the majority report illustrate the views of employers during a period of depression as represented by one of the major employers' organizations. The majority report's conclusions followed this line fairly closely. The minority report continued to reflect the more optimistic line of the pre-war period.

Evidence as to the burden on industry
We have heard evidence from the National Confederation of Employers' Organizations on this aspect of the problem (Q. 24, 543–24, 548), and we direct attention also to the statement which they have submitted to us (App. CVII). That confederation claims to speak authoritatively on behalf of the employers of the country, as it is a central body representative of the various great federations whose constituent members have in the aggregate an employment roll of about seven million workers. The witnesses informed us that the confederation is recognized by the government as the mouthpiece of the employers on all matters affecting the latter's industrial relations to their workpeople; and that it nominates each year, on the invitation of Your Majesty's Government, the delegates and technical advisers to represent British employers at the International Labour Conference at Geneva held under Part XIII of the Treaty of Peace.

From this organization, as will be seen from the evidence, we have received the strongest representations that industry cannot bear any further burden at present, and, indeed, that the need for some alleviation of the load is most urgent and could be readily realized by a substantial reduction of the contributions of employers and employed persons under the health insurance scheme. They maintain 'that there is a definite limit to the amount of money which any country can afford to spend in the providing of social services', and that 'that limit has in Great Britain already been largely exceeded, and particularly so in the case of health insurance' (App. CVII, 6). They submit the following table to illustrate the relative position in the principal European countries and to show how heavy in comparison is the burden imposed on Great Britain in respect of five of the social services, viz. poor law, workmen's compensation, old-age pensions, health insurance and unemployment insurance:

	Country	Cost of five social services per head of total population	
		Actual	Per cent as compared with Great Britain
		s d	
1	Great Britain	78 6	100 per cent
2	Germany	37 6	48 ,,
3	France	13 0	17 ,,
4	Czechoslovakia	11 0	14 ,,
5	Belgium	5 6	7 ,,
6	Italy	3 6	4 ,,

General conclusion

In concluding this brief review of the present financial burden of the social services, we desire to make it clear that we do not in any way deprecate or condemn either the volume or the application of that expenditure. A civilized nation must carry the burdens of civilization; and prosperity – even material prosperity – fulfils itself in many ways. America, for example, though devoting great resources to public education and other general services, makes little or no public provision for social insurance. Being able to pay high rates of wages in consequence of her unique economic position, she leaves the provision against the individual casualties of life to the personal and voluntary effort of her workers. Our country, on the other hand, has chosen, and rightly as we think, to make several great schemes of social insurance an integral and permanent part of the national life. But while this principle may be accepted, it is clearly essential that a balance between the expenditure on these schemes and the productive capacity of the country should, from time to time, be struck, even though this can probably be done only in a very general way and without reduction to any precise formula, of which, indeed, the conditions do not permit. If, ignoring such considerations of prudence, the rate of expenditure outruns in a substantial way the productive capacity of the country, the result must surely be to stultify the aims which the nation has set before itself. It is small consolation to a bankrupt to be told that his doctor's bills have been the main cause of his disaster.

These considerations are, we think, relevant to our reference in view of the wide and costly extensions of the health insurance scheme which have been urged on us from many quarters. We have every sympathy for such proposals and every desire that this country should maintain that leadership in the provision of social services which it has certainly shown to the world. At the same time we feel that there may come a time, and that in fact there has come a time, when the state may justifiably turn from searching its conscience to exploring its purse, and that in connexion with our present reference we are entitled to direct attention to this grave problem, and to frame our recommendations in the light – or the darkness – of the economic condition of the nation.

We therefore make the definite recommendation that only such extensions or modifications as involve no expenditure or can be met within the present financial resources of the scheme, should be considered as immediately practicable. This implies that, in our opinion, there should be no increase at the present time in the rates of contribution under the scheme. We consider also that the scheme should be self-supporting subject to the payment by the exchequer of its present proportionate share of the cost of benefits and their administration, together with the cost of the general supervision of the scheme by the ministry of health and the Scottish board of health. We recommend that beyond these charges no further liability should rest on the Exchequer in any circumstances. This would involve the repeal of the provision of the act under which the exchequer is contingently liable to make a contribution to the central fund.

Royal Commission on National Health Insurance, Cmd. 2596 (1926)

31   Employers: The Beveridge Report, 1942

The next three documents illustrate the divisions in the ranks of employers over welfare and social reform during the second world war. The majority in the British Employers Confederation took the view that social services should be directly related to the industrial performance of the country and should not weaken incentives to work. No promises should be made until the post-war state of the country was clear.

In the building up of our state insurance systems for unemployment, health and pensions, the confederation has supported the principle of a national compulsory contributory system as an integral part of our industrial life.

In its evidence before the various commissions and committees, the confederation has often had occasion to criticize the operation and development of these systems but it has never failed to recognize the beneficial part which these services, under proper safeguards, are qualified to play in the welfare of this industrial country.

The confederation has throughout, however, maintained that it is imperative that the expenditure on these services, and the other social services, must be directly related to the industrial performance of the country on which they ultimately depend for their continuance, and that the benefits they provide should not be such as to weaken the incentive of the population to play their full part in maintaining the productivity and exporting ability of the country.

In the view of the confederation, the ignoring of these fundamental principles and the consequent reaction on our production costs aggravated in no small measure the industrial depression and its resultant unemployment which characterized British industry for so many years after the last war and which culminated in the economic crisis of 1931.

In expressing that view, the confederation had in mind that this country had to depend more than any other on its industries for the providing of employment for its people; that to keep these industries in operation and maintain the life of its people, this country was more dependent than any other on its ability to purchase raw materials and food from abroad; and that, in order to pay for these imports, it had to rely more than any other country on the competitive ability of its industries to sell their products abroad.

As showing the critical dependence of this country on its industries for the providing of employment, it may be noted that, before the present war, the percentage of the occupied population in Great

Britain engaged in industry and commerce – as distinct from agriculture – was 93 per cent, whereas in USA it was only 78 per cent, in Germany 69 per cent, in France 62 per cent, in Japan 46 per cent, and in Italy 44 per cent.

As showing the critical dependence of this country on its ability to purchase food and raw materials from abroad, it may be noted that, before the present war, the cost of these imports by Great Britain represented £14 5s per head of its population and that – taking Great Britain as 100 – the comparative figure for other countries was France 38, Germany 33, USA 13, Italy 12, Japan 8.

In the light of these considerations, the confederation regards it as essential in the first place that any proposals for a new or revised social services system to operate after the present war should be framed with due regard to the potential post-war economic position of the country. . . .

Such defects as have crept into our social service system are in large measure due to the fact that, in the origin and growth of these services as separate entities, there has been no central planning authority responsible for maintaining a true sense of perspective.

Further, it is true to say that in many cases the development of the individual services has been dominated by political considerations arising from the programmes which the various political parties have from time to time placed before their constituents.

It was with that in mind that the confederation, in its evidence before the Royal Commission on Unemployment Insurance in 1931, recommended the setting up of a statutory body charged with the responsibility of maintaining the solvency of the unemployment insurance fund.

The recommendation was given effect to in the setting up of the Unemployment Insurance Statutory Committee and the success which has attended the work of that committee causes the confederation now to make a wider proposal.

The proposal is that this country should now envisage, as part of its post-war planning, a permanent commission which would be responsible for overseeing the social services of the country as a whole and making recommendations to the Government on their development in much the same way as the Unemployment Insurance Statutory Committee at present does to the ministry of labour and national service with regard to unemployment insurance.

With that as the ultimate goal, the confederation suggests that there should meanwhile be set up a small wartime commission which would form the nucleus for that permanent post-war body and which, by keeping this complex problem under continuous review from now on and while post-war possibilities are more clearly emerging, would be in a position to have ready by the end of the war, for the consideration of those concerned, the draft scheme or schemes most likely to fit in with the post-war situation.

As we have explained in this memorandum, the present urgency of war production makes it physically impossible for employers and their organizations to devote to this complex problem the time and attention which any comprehensive study of it would entail.

We further hold the view that such a large scale diversion of the attention of industry from its war production problems to the study of a post-war problem which must inevitably be highly speculative at this stage would be out of keeping with the statement which the Prime Minister made in the Caxton Hall on 27th March last when he said: 'We must be, above all things, careful that nothing diverts or distracts our thoughts or our fullest energies from the task of national self-preservation and of inter-allied duty which will require the total concentration for an indefinite period of all that we can give.'

Memorandum from British Employers Confederation, Social Insurance and Allied Services, Cmd. 6405 (1942)

32   Employers: The positive case for welfare, 1942

1   This country is entitled to feel proud of its social services as a whole.

The individual services have come in for a good deal of criticism. Much of this is because they have grown up piece-meal, and have been allowed to develop in an apparently haphazard fashion. One of the compensations of this method of development is that it has enabled many experiments to be made. But the experimental stage is now over and for some years employers have urged that, instead of individual reviews in watertight compartments, the social services should be surveyed as a whole. We therefore welcome this opportunity of putting their suggestions before the inter-departmental committee.

2   It seems to us that the present social services are like an industry in need of rationalization. They are wastefully competitive: their products are not sufficiently standardized: their plants are too numerous and some are out-of-date.

3   Our main proposal is that there should be a single national

compulsory contributory industrial social insurance scheme embracing the industrial risks now covered by the following four separate schemes:

(a) Unemployment;
(b) health insurance;
(c) workmen's compensation;
(d) widows, orphans and old-age pensions

The new scheme should be financed by equal contibutions from employers and employees and by at least an equal third from the exchequer. There should be a single combined weekly contribution from employer and employed covering all four services.

The cash benefits should be the same for the first three risks and (unless a more generous scheme of family allowances finds favour) should provide for family benefits.

The medical benefits should be the same for accident, disease and illness, wherever they occur, i.e. irrespective of whether or not they are due to the fact of employment and should be available to the dependants of the insured.

There should be a single administrative collecting agency and, probably, also a single payment agency.

There should continue to be separate administrative agencies for placing in employment and for administering medical benefits.

To supervise the scheme as a whole there should be a special statutory committee or body of social service commissioners.

4   To avoid a morass of detail this memorandum is confined to broad general outlines.

On finance, in particular, it is only possible to deal in general principles, because we cannot foretell what we will be able to afford for the social services after the war.

> Memorandum of Evidence by the Shipping
> Federation and the Liverpool Steam Ship
> Owners' Association, Social Insurance and
> Allied Services, Cmd. 6405 (1942)

33   A national policy for industry, 1942

These proposals are taken from a statement prepared by 120 leading industrialists, led by Lord McGowan of ICI.

Industry should accept a 'code of duty' towards employees under which –

(a) Workers should have full opportunities for promotion.

(b) There should be a minimum basic wage.

(c) To avoid unemployment, industry might be subsidized after consultation by the government with the relevant trade associations.

(d) Sickness and disability allowances should be such as to free the recipient from want when incapacitated from these causes.

(e) Holidays with pay should be established throughout industry.

(f) Reasonable hours of work should be agreed for all industrial workers according to the nature of their work and other relevant circumstances.

(g) 'We are in favour of a scheme of family allowances for children up to the school-leaving age.'

(h) State old-age pensions should be supplemented by pension schemes operated by private firms.

(j) 'We regard it as the ultimate duty of industry to ensure that its own employees are properly housed on reasonable terms.'

(k) The school-leaving age should be raised to 16 and there should be part-time compulsory education up to the age of 18. Industry should give much more thought to schemes for industrial and vocational education, training and promotion, so that every employee with the requisite capacity may be able to fit himself for higher responsibilities.

Charles Madge, Industry After the War (1943),
35

III

Welfare and the experts: the role of social investigators, social workers and civil servants

34 Henry Mayhew: Poverty and politics, 1849

Mayhew's pioneering work as a social investigator merits comparison with that of Booth and Rowntree. Here he notes the effects of irregular employment on unskilled labourers and outlines the political opinions of various working-class groups.

Regularity of habits are incompatible with irregularity of income; indeed, the very conditions necessary for the formation of any habit whatsoever are that the act or thing to which we are to become habituated should be repeated at frequent and regular intervals. It is a moral impossibility that the class of labourers who are only occasionally employed should be either generally industrious or temperate – both industry and temperance being habits produced by constancy of employment and uniformity of income. Hence, where the greatest fluctuation occurs in the labour, there, of course, will be the greatest idleness and improvidence; where the greatest want generally is, there we shall find the greatest occasional excess; where from the uncertainty of the occupation prudence is most needed, there, strange to say, we shall meet with the highest improvidence of all. . . .

It seems as if we were in a new land, and among another race. The artisans are almost to a man red-hot politicians. They are sufficiently educated and thoughtful to have a sense of their importance in the state. . . . They begin to view their class, not as a mere isolated body of workmen, but as an integral portion of the nation, contributing their quota to the general welfare. If property has its duties as well as its rights; labour, on the other hand, they say, has its rights as well as its duties. . . .

The unskilled labourers are a different class of people. As yet they are as unpolitical as footmen, and instead of entertaining violent democratic opinions, they appear to have no political opinions whatever; or, if they do possess any, they rather lead towards the maintenance of 'things as they are', than towards the ascendancy of the working people. I have lately been investigating the state of the coalwhippers and these reflections are forced upon me by the marked difference in the character and sentiments of these people from those of the operative tailors. Among the latter class there appeared to be a general bias towards the six points of the Charter; but the former were extremely proud of their having turned out to a man on the 10th of April 1848 and become special constables for the maintenance of law and order on the great day of the great Chartist demonstration.

> Henry Mayhew, *Morning Chronicle* (1849), from E. P. Thompson and E. Yeo, *The Unknown Mayhew* (1973 edn), 94-5

35   Alfred Marshall: The way to prevent the abuse of outdoor relief, 1893

These are an economist's suggestions for improving the administration of the Poor Law to reduce malingering.

Then you were making a suggestion that the Charity Organization Society should work with the Poor Law guardians with regard to the administration of outdoor relief; do you desire that the Charity Organization Society should be changed from a purely voluntary association; that it would be set up by legal enactment, to act with the guardians? – I should desire that although where the Charity Organization Society is strong in men and women, and money, as it is in certain places, for instance in Oxford, and to a less extent in Cambridge, there, I take it, no change can make any considerable improvement. The only change that needs to be made in such cases is one that would enable working men to take a direct part in the administration of relief. I am convinced – for I have made inquiries on the subject from representative working men – I am convinced that the leaders of the working men would be as firm as anyone in insisting that scamps and lazy people should be put to a severe discipline; that they would be in many ways sharper than people not in the same rank of life in seeing through a fallacious story, and would have no sympathy at all with the tramp; in fact I believe that probably the professional tramp is

even more odious to large classes of the working men then he is to the
rest of society.

A. Marshall, Evidence to Royal Commission
on Aged Poor (1893), from J. M. Keynes (ed),
Official Papers by Alfred Marshall (1926), 210

36   Alfred Marshall: The economic effects of old-age pensions, 1893

One commonly expressed fear in the nineteenth century was that old-age
pensions would tend to force down wages by bringing subsidized workers into
competition with independent workers. Marshall's analogy is famous,
apposite and often forgotten. It was also delivered to the Royal Commission
on the Aged Poor.

What you have said today I take to have been entirely with regard to the
general effect of money provided by the rich for the poor; and what I
want to ask you is whether there is not a special possible effect on wages
due to the active competition of subsidized individuals. I think that
anything that increases the supply of labour in any particular market
tends to force down real wages in the market, but tends also to raise the
real wages of the people who produce the things consumed in the
market; therefore, I think that if a certain number of old men who are
now considered past work are to be added to the ranks of effective
labourers all over the country that would have the effect of increasing
the general well-being of the working classes. While I admit that if they
are there disproportionately in any particular trade they would tend to
cause a glut of the things produced in that trade and that trade only,
though possibly to the greater benefit often of other trades.

You do not think that more old people would come into
competition for work if they had an allowance of public money? – Not
necessarily. May I put the case in this way: suppose you could conceive
a mad emperor of China to give to every English working man half-a-
crown for nothing: according to the current notions, so far as I have
been able to ascertain them, that would lower wages, because it would
enable people to work for less. I think that nine economists out of ten
at the beginning of the century would have said that that would lower
wages. Well, of course, it might increase population, and that might
bring down wages; but unless it did increase population, the effect
according to the modern school would be to raise wages because the
increased wealth of the working classes would lead to better living,
more vigorous and better educated people, with greater earning

power, and so wages would rise. That is the centre of the difference.

Alfred Marshall, *Official Papers*, ed. J. M.
Keynes (1926), 248–9

37   Charles Booth: Poverty, 1897

Booth was concerned with both the economic and what he saw as the moral causes of poverty. This brief extract brings out the tenuous connection between the level of wages, overcrowding and poverty.

On the whole, reviewing all the facts before us, it seems probable that the line of poverty in London, if we are to accept crowding as a test, lies a little above the figure formerly laid down. . . .

It must be admitted, however, that the relationship between the statistics of remuneration and those of poverty as tested by crowding is not very close. The discrepancies may be explained and bridged over, but they remain in many ways more remarkable than the agreement which underlies them. One thing is abundantly evident, that the full amount of nominal wages does not, as a rule, reach the home. Some proportion is either not received at all or else is dissipated in some way in a sufficient number of cases to materially affect the averages. Between these two great causes of domestic poverty – irregularity of earning and irregularity of conduct, both of which act in the same direction – it is not possible to divide very exactly the responsibility for impoverished homes. According to the bent of one's mind or the mood of the moment, greater importance is attached to this cause or that, and the onlooker remembers the uncertainties of work or dwells upon the recklessness of expenditure, and especially of expenditure in drink. Moreover, these causes are complicated by interaction. A man is apt to drink when he is idle, as well as to lose his work because of intemperate habits.

A valuable comparison might be made between the economic position of families more or less uniform in size known to be earning about the same money; such a comparison would undoubtedly show an amazing divergence, rapidly increasing as time went on and self-restraint and good management showed its cumulative effect. Some families can never save on any income, while others succeed in doing so, however limited may be their means. Moreover, what is true of savings is also true of all that is obtained for money spent; the decency and comfort of the home, the quality of the food eaten, and the perfection or imperfection of the clothes worn, are by no means necessarily in proportion to amount earned. On all these points successful results are possible even with very straitened means if the man is loyal and the woman prudent, while they are unattainable without these virtues, even when the earnings are much larger; and it may be noticed that wise spending and wise saving go usually hand in hand.

It is not my object now to discuss the moral bearings of the questions. I merely point them out in order to account in part for the divergency between earnings and what is shown for them on the average in many trades.

C. Booth, *Life and Labour of the People of London*
IX (1897), 25–7

38   Seebohm Rowntree: The cycle of poverty, 1901

Rowntree's investigation of poverty in York broke new ground in various ways including this appreciation that poverty varied over the life cycle of any family group.

The life of a labourer is marked by five alternating periods of want and comparative plenty. During early childhood, unless his father is a skilled worker, he probably will be in poverty; this will last until he, or some of his brothers or sisters, begin to earn money and thus augment their father's wage sufficiently to raise the family above the poverty line. Then follows the period during which he is earning money and living under his parents' roof; for some portion of this period he will be earning more money than is required for lodging, food, and clothes. This is his chance to save money. If he has saved enough to pay for furnishing a cottage, the period of comparative prosperity may continue after marriage until he has two or three children, when poverty will again overtake him. This period of poverty will last perhaps for ten years, i.e. until the first child is fourteen years old and begins to earn wages; but if there are more than three children it may last longer. While the children are earning, and before they leave the home to marry, the man enjoys another period of prosperity – possibly, however, only to sink back again into poverty when his children have married and left him, and he himself is too old to work, for his income has never permitted his saving enough for him and his wife to live upon for more than a very short time.

A labourer is thus in poverty, and therefore underfed –

(a) In childhood – when his constitution is being built up.

(b) In early middle life – when he should be in his prime.
(c) In old age.

The accompanying diagram may serve to illustrate this:

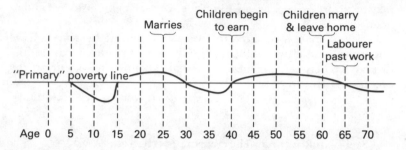

It should be noted that the women are in poverty during the greater part of the period that they are bearing children.

We thus see that the 7,230 persons shown by this inquiry to be in a state of 'primary' poverty represent merely that section who happened to be in one of these poverty periods at the time the inquiry was made.

S. Rowntree, *Poverty: A Study of Town Life* (1901), 136–7

39   Margaret MacMillan: School meals, 1900s

Margaret MacMillan was a pioneer of school meals in Bradford where she worked closely with the Independent Labour Party. Her work had some influence on politicians and civil servants like Sir Robert Morant, Permanent Secretary of the Board of Education, 1903–11.

Feeding of school children – Margaret never tired of arguing that it was wasting money to try to educate a hungry, let alone a starving, child.

The state compels the children to work [in school] – it makes the demand for sustenance urgent, intolerable.

But it does not compel parents to feed their children. Hence it is certain to some of these hungry little ones free education is less of a boon than an outrage.

Here, for example, is a group of very hopeful children. They have known what hunger is all their lives, but never have they been so hungry as now. When they were little they used to get scraps of food, and now and again a good meal, and this was enough to allow them to live a free, careless life in the fields or alleys. But at last the school board officer got on their track. They were led into a big school, and obliged to read, write, sing, calculate. Not one of these processes but involves a quickening of all the life processes, a new expenditure at a definite rate of nervous energy and living tissue. Lo! at noon all the children are ravenously hungry. The thought that dinner is a movable feast – that there is no dinner to be had – is now a dreadful one! Yesterday's hunger is a mild thing compared with today's.

> Albert Mansbridge, *Margaret MacMillan, Prophet and Pioneer* (1932), 41–2

40 Robert Morant: The physical condition of schoolchildren, 1906

Morant refers to the influence of Margaret MacMillan on his plans to introduce medical and physiological improvements in schools.

I have for some time past come to feel that for the good of the children and the public, what subjects are taught and how much they are taught *do not matter anything like so much nowadays* as attention (a) to the *physical* condition of the scholars and the teacher and (b) to the physiological aspect of the school. . . .

Between us we shall do something, I am sure, if we can avoid raising a public hubbub against our efforts, and I have found it an immense help to have a talk with you. I trust we may have many more together.

> A. Mansbridge, *Margaret MacMillan, Prophet and Pioneer* (1932), from B. B. Gilbert, *The Evolution of National Insurance in Great Britain* (1966), 129

41 The Treasury: Expenditure on school meals, 1906

Hamilton was permanent secretary to the Treasury. He was a firm 'Gladstonian' on financial matters and believed that expensive social welfare would lead inevitably to the success of the tariff reform movement. Yet he was also concerned with the efficiency of British society.

The H. of Commons passed a bill yesterday in favour of feeding children at the schools. It is very idealistic and this is how the money will go; but there is much to be said against educating children on an empty stomach.

> Sir Edward Hamilton's Diary (Saturday 4 March 1906), British Museum, Additional Manuscripts, 48683

42   Sir Robert Morant: Medical inspection of schoolchildren, 1906

Morant, the Permanent Secretary of the Board of Education, managed to introduce medical inspection under the Education (Administrative Provisions) Act of 1907.

Morant knew . . . but did not tell his minister, that medical inspection would reveal such a mass of disease and defect that no government subsequently would be able to resist the demand of the local education authorities to provide treatment. Morant told me himself that he foresaw what would happen and *meant it to happen* because without the horrifying results of inspection there was no chance for a bill authorizing treatment. Up to this time the state had not provided treatment, except under the Poor Law, for anything but infectious diseases. . . .

It was Morant's action that broke down the barrier established by the Public Health Act of 1875. He started and set in motion a vast social revolution probably without then foreseeing the ultimate result of his action.

Violet Markham, *Friendship's Harvest* (1956),
200–201, from B. B. Gilbert, *The Evolution of*
National Insurance in Great Britain (1966), 128–9

43   Beatrice Webb: The politics of influence, 1908

The personal and professional connections between experts, civil servants and politicians were often extremely close. The Webbs' characterization of their role is interesting, though their estimate of their influence cannot be accepted at face value.

Dinner with Haldane, at which I went in with Asquith, and had some talk with Winston Churchill – renewed our acquaintance; dining tonight with Sydney Buxton and on Monday with Asquith and seeing such folk as Masterman, Lyttelton and other MPs. The net impression left on our mind is the scramble for new constructive ideas. We happen just now to have a good many to give away, hence the eagerness for our company. Every politician one meets wants to be coached – it is really quite comic – it seems to be quite irrelevant whether they are Conservatives, Liberals or Labour Party men – all alike have become mendicants for practicable proposals. Hence, our life has become somewhat too exciting. We have the hard grind of the Poor Law enquiry and, on the top of it, speculative investments in the minds of rival politicians. We are inclined to plunge heavily in all parties, give freely to anyone who comes along – the more the merrier. . . .

Meanwhile, Morant has provided me with some hundred copies of my scheme for breaking up the Poor Law, which he has had printed for his own consideration. I have sent or given it in confidence to Asquith, Lloyd George, Haldane, Winston Churchill, McKenna, Sydney Buxton, Runciman, Harcourt, H. Samuel, John Burns, McKinnon Wood of the present government, and Balfour, Long, Austen Chamberlain, Lyttelton, Gerald Balfour of the late government, and to a select few important civil servants, journalists and local administrators. I have a notion that, when we have got our 'unemployed' scheme drafted in its final form, we will get Winston Churchill to print it at the Board of Trade and do ditto with that. Such big schemes require careful consideration by many brains, they have to sink in to the minds of those likely to carry them out, if they are to become practical politics within a generation.

B. Webb, Our Partnership (1948), 402 and
410–11

44 Beveridge: The analysis of unemployment, 1909

Beveridge contributed in his work and his writing to the idea that unemployment was primarily an industrial and national problem rather than one of personal character and local maladjustments in supply and demand. His analysis here does not allow for a deficiency of aggregate demand in the sense envisaged by Keynes.

At the threshold, therefore, of the present inquiry lies the general question as to the relations of population and industry. Until the bearings of that are known, discussion of particular types of unemployment is useless. Consideration of it involves a brief examination of general social conditions and tendencies today.

There are, no doubt, economic forces which tend in the long run to adjust supply and demand in regard to labour as in regard to all other commodities. The supply of labour, even in the most general sense – that of population – is influenced by the state of the demand.

This process of adjustment, moreover, is not and cannot be checked in the long run by deficiency in the demand for the products of labour. The total demand for these products must be regarded as infinite or at least as capable of indefinite expansion. It is impossible to imagine a state of affairs in which every need for material good things was satisfied and labour idle because nothing remained to be done. Least of all could such a description apply to a society in which men were seeking employment; the very fact of their seeking employment would show that some of their demands for commodities were unsatisfied. Over-production of any one particular good thing is possible and not uncommon. Over-production of all the good things of life is, strictly speaking, an impossibility. The satisfaction of one need is followed by the immediate growth of another; the standard of comfort can and does rise indefinitely.

These general economic arguments have their place in the present discussion. They do not, however, carry the matter very far. They leave the field clear for two distinct objections. First, the forces which make for equilibrium in the labour market, though ultimately they cannot be limited through deficient demand for commodities, may yet be limited in other ways. Second, these forces make only for ultimate equilibrium; they get to work very slowly and never complete their work.

W. H. Beveridge, *Unemployment: A Problem of Industry* (1909), 4–5

45   Norman Pearson: The control of the idle poor, 1911

'National efficiency' and social Darwinist arguments in the hands of middle-class writers could often lead to very different conclusions from those of document 47 as this extract shows.

It is to be feared that the confirmed loafer and the habitual vagrant are seldom capable of being reformed. It is a mistake to suppose that the typical pauper is merely an ordinary person who has fallen into distress through adverse circumstances. As a rule he is not an ordinary person, but one who is constitutionally a pauper, a pauper in his blood and bones. He is made of inferior material, and therefore cannot be improved up to the level of the ordinary person. It is not suggested that pauperism *per se* is capable of hereditary transmission as a definite integral quality; but it is clearly, to a great extent, the outcome of qualities which can be so transmitted. Speaking broadly, pauperism is a token of the inferior capacity which belongs to an inferior stock. The hereditary nature of this incapacity may lighten the moral reproach against the loafer and the vagrant, but it emphasizes the necessity of protecting the community against them, and, in particular, of protecting it against the perpetuation of the degenerate stocks which they represent.

This is an aspect of the case which, till lately, has been too much overlooked, but it is really the most important factor in the problem, seeing that it affects not only ourselves but our prosperity. On this ground alone the proper authorities should be invested with the power of segregating and detaining – permanently, if necessary – those who burden the present and imperil the future of our race.

Norman Pearson, 'The Idle Poor', *Nineteenth
Century and After*, 70 (1911), 917

46   John MacCunn: Motives to social work, 1911

An early analysis of the reasons for the growth of social work. MacCunn was a professor of philosophy, and his detailed analysis should be compared with documents 40, 42, 43 and 47.

It is no disparagement of human nature to say, to begin with, that of these motives one is fear. This, indeed, is only what one might expect. For most movements for social betterment have, as their shadow, an element of menace. In other words, they are commonly accompanied by pictures, sometimes highly rhetorical, sometimes conjured up by the unadorned eloquence of facts, of the miseries, hardships, and wrongs that need redress, and forecasts, sometimes threatening enough, of what will happen if nothing is done. And these forebodings – for society never lacks its Cassandras – take many forms. Early in the nineteenth century the alarm was political revolution. Then, under Malthusian influence, it was over-population. Nowadays, when biology and physiology have had their say, it is rather physical and moral degeneracy and the congested squalor of great cities. But there are, of course, many alarms besides these, alarms of industrial conflict, failure of employment, commercial defeat, pauperism, attacks on property, decay of the family, popular ignorance, intemperance, inordinate luxury, decline of national character, religious infidelity, and so on. Nor, in view of the grim catalogue, is it too much to say that in the nineteenth century democracy has come into its kingdom – to find that its kingdom is a *damnosa hereditas* of difficulties that seem likely to put it to the proof. It is a natural result that many persons, and by no means only those who are pessimists or alarmists, go about haunted by all manner of vague fears of impending catastrophes.

Now it need not be suggested that these vague fears have ever of themselves done much to prompt social work. General alarms are singularly impotent to create concrete service. Did fear of national degeneracy ever yet produce an officer of health? Did fear of pauperism ever yet inspire a single guardian of the poor? And yet fear has its place: indirectly, and in association with other things, it is certainly far from impotent.

One may see this in politics and legislation. Fear for the future of one's country, it has been well said, is heroic virtue; and so must it ever be, so long as it is no small part of the statesman's work to dissipate alarms and restore confidence. More potent still is the fear that attaches itself to some definite institution that is believed to be in danger. Conspicuously so when menaces rouse the strong resentful instincts of alarmed resistance. The instinct may be often enough unreasoning and obstructive; but that is no ground for denying it the title to be ranked as a motive to social work. Especially, of course, when the threatened institution is one that has enlisted time-honoured loyalties and affections. Let but a man's church be assailed, or his trading company, or his trades union, or his school or university – does not indifference shake off its apathy and develop a militant energy that astonishes the world? It would be sheer blindness to overlook the volume of passion and effort that is poured into public questions by the conservative instincts of society; and in these conservative instincts fear is no small element. Let none withhold his tribute from even the champions of lost causes. They have not lived in vain, even if they have done no more than stir the stagnant waters of political apathy.

And yet, when fear thus plays its part, it need not receive more than its due. For that part is after all but partial, because it is only the negative side of a positive loyalty and attachment to institutions. It is this that gives substance, this that nerves it to effort and sustains it in work; this that makes all the difference between the mere political nervousness which fears it knows not what, and the fear which has become a just solicitude for the fate of something a man believes worth having and living for. The truth is that human affairs are always sufficiently precarious to render it impossible to care much for anything without some dash of fears. Nor is the best citizen the man with the fewest fears for his country's institutions. But with him the fear is only the shadow; the loyalty, the attachment, is the substance.

Fortunately *this* motive – this positive loyalty and attachment to institutions – is one upon which in most countries, and in none more than our own, we can confidently reckon. Its object may vary. It may be a village club or a political party; a local school or a national church. But in one form or another the motive is widespread, persistent, and effective.

John MacCunn, *Liverpool Addresses on the Ethics of Social Work (1911)*, 4–8

47 R. C. K. Ensor: 'The national efficiency' argument for a minimum wage, 1912

Ensor, Fabian and later historian of this period, puts the case for a legal minimum wage. Notice the use of social, economic and political arguments to support the positive intervention of the state and contrast this with document 45.

If the labour unrest of these days indicates a disease in society – and among thinking people there cannot be much doubt that it does – then it will not be enough to prescribe merely for the surface symptoms. Many people talk about strikes as if the matter began and ended with some flaw in the machinery of collective bargaining or some supposed weakness of the police in dealing with pickets. One physician wants trade unions strengthened, another wants them smashed; one advises compulsory arbitration, another that voluntary agreements be given the force of law; a fifth longs to repeal the Trade Disputes Act; a sixth has still faith in the elixir of rifles and bayonets. All of these prescriptions cannot be beneficial and valuable alike, though some may be so to a high degree. But it is important to go behind them and consider the hygiene of the patient. It is as part of such a policy of social hygiene, not tinkering directly with the symptoms of labour disputes, but strengthening broadly the forces which make for social peace and stability, that the policy of a legally enforced minimum wage has today a special claim on the attention of moderate and far-seeing statesmen.

Anyone who inquires seriously into the present discontents must be struck by an emphatic and remarkable coincidence between the testimony of the social investigator and that of the insurgent workman upon a single point. That point is the under-payment of the lower-paid workers. The coal strike of last spring was typical of the workmen's attitude towards this; the whole body of men in our largest trade organization left work, not to secure any general advance of wages or alteration of hours for their members, but solely that the worst-paid men and grades (quite a minority of the whole) should be benefited, and that no one employed should, from no fault of his own, earn less than a fixed minimum wage. The same idea prompts the demand, which the Labour Party has urged on parliament, for a 'national minimum wage of 30s a week for all workers', a demand perhaps crude and impracticable enough when stated in order to strike the eye, and, at any rate, containing an interesting kernel of principle. It may be affirmed with confidence that throughout the world of labour at present the emphasis is on this same point; and the results of social investigation show plenty of reason why it should be. We all know the findings of Mr Booth and Mr Seebohm Rowntree – how in London in 1891 30·7 per cent of the people were calculated, and in York in 1902 27·84 per cent were actually ascertained, to be living on incomes below a physiological minimum. These figures would probably understate the case today; for the last ten years have witnessed a steep rise in the cost of working-class living, and scarcely any rise of wages, except some that in the last fifteen months have been obtained by striking. The thirteen millions of whom the late Sir Henry Campbell-Bannerman said seven or eight years ago that they were constantly 'on the verge of hunger', are almost certainly more numerous and hungrier now than they were then.

Now, forgetting for a moment the part which this underpayment may play in generating a blind and destructive type of social discontent, let us look purely at its economics, and ask what happens, when wages are paid too low to sustain physical efficiency, at least after the minimum demands of civilized custom have been satisfied. One of two things happens: either physical efficiency is not sustained, and the underpaying industry is actually eating into the capital value of the worker; or else it is sustained, but only because to make up the deficiency in the wages of the underpaid worker part of the wages paid by some other industry is brought in (as when an underpaid tailoress is housed for nothing by her parents, or an underpaid carman relies on the earnings of his daughters in a cotton-mill), or relatives are diverted from non-industrial duties to wage-earning (as when the underpaid carman's wife neglects her children to go out laundering, or his children of school age sell newspapers in the streets). In either case the underpaying industry is, in the strict economic sense, parasitic. In the first and last cases it levies a tax on the community at large; in the second case it levies one on some other special industry or industries. Neither way is it any less bounty-fed, unfairly advantaged industry than one to which state bounties are paid over in hard cash, as to the beet-sugar industry of the Continent. Indeed, a system of state bounties is far less objectionable; for the amount of the bounty is definite and visible and it comes from general taxation, whose burdens may be distributed as equitably as the nation chooses; whereas the bounty received by an industry which pays less than subsistence wages is indefinite and elusive, its burdens are laid at random, largely on the weakest shoulders, and the nation foots the bill, not in money only, but in physical deterioration, moral degradation, and social catastrophe.

This being so, such underpayment tends clearly to the loss of the nation; and it is difficult on any ground of pure logic to see why the state, as trustee of the national interests, should not interfere with it, just as it has interfered with other features in the competitive industry which appeared destructive of the nation's human capital.

> R. C. K. Ensor, 'The Practical Case for a Legal
> Minimum Wage', *Nineteenth Century and After*
> 72 (1912), 264–6

48   Tom Jones: Industrial unrest and social reform, 1919

Jones was deputy secretary to the Cabinet. In this memorandum, written just after the strike for a forty-hour week which ended in riots in George Square in Glasgow, Jones urges David Lloyd George, the Prime Minister, to embark on a social reform programme as an antidote to social and political unrest.

1   Bolshevik propaganda in this country is only dangerous in so far as it can lodge itself in the soil of genuine grievances. There is no doubt that large numbers of workpeople are expecting a big and rapid improvement in their social and industrial conditions. They are disturbed by all sorts of rumours, usually exaggerated, that the surplus factories and stores of the government are being handed over at ridiculously low prices to the profit-makers.

2   Much of the present difficulty springs from the mutiny of the rank and file against the old established leaders and there seems to be no machinery for bringing about a quick change of leaders. Working men are notoriously tender towards the man in office and most unwilling to sack him, however incompetent or out of touch. The government's decision to stand by the accredited leaders is the only possible policy but it does not get over the fact that the leaders no longer represent the more active and agitating minds in the labour movement.

3   A definite reiteration by yourself of the government's determination to push forward with an advanced social programme is the best antidote, and this should be followed up by instructions from

you to the departments concerned to get on with the necessary bills at top speed.

Sir Robert Horne yesterday suggested at the War Cabinet that a fresh series of local commissions on industrial unrest should be set up like those you appointed a couple of years ago. I think this device too thin. We have not carried out the recommendations of the last series. What is wanted is real, concrete proposals from the departments and these to be pushed through the House. The Whitley Councils are coming into existence and they should be appealed to and asked to meet at once and consider improvements in the conditions of their respective industries.

(a) Hours. Could the government not bring in an eight-hours bill for the main organized industries (except agriculture) and then allow exemptions to be granted by licence?

(b) Wages. The miners are demanding 30 per cent on pre-war earnings and 18s war bonus. The railwaymen are putting forward fresh demands. I think you should say frankly that the government is unwilling to commit itself to these big advances to the highest paid workers (and thereby create an industrial House of Lords) until more has been done to secure a national minimum for the lower paid in these two industries and for those in the low skilled and unskilled industries: that therefore you contemplate an immediate extension of the trade boards in order to secure the enforcement of this national minimum.

(c) Housing. It would be helpful if you gave a summary of the enormous tenders that the minister of supply has put out. The figures are impressive.

You should tell the big municipalities (e.g. Glasgow) that you hope they will tackle the re-housing of their cities with something of the wartime energy that you shewed at the Ministry of Munitions. We do not want to wait twenty years for these houses. Hundreds of thousands should be put up in the next five years.

Tom Jones, *Whitehall Diary* I, 1916–25 (1969)

49   Pilgrim Trust enquiry into unemployment in the 1930s

The enquiry probed the statistics of unemployment to try to find out what it was like to experience unemployment. This extract refers to differences between 'white' and 'blue' collar workers.

One of the main differences between the 'working' classes and the 'middle' classes is the difference of security. This is probably a more important distinction than income level. If working men and women seem to be unduly anxious to make their sons and daughters into clerks, the anxiety behind it is not for more money but for greater security. Rightly or wrongly, they feel that the black-coated worker has a more assured position. The semi-skilled man is at the mercy of rationalization. A week's notice may end half a lifetime's service, with no prospects, if he is elderly, but the dole, followed by a still further reduction in his means of livelihood when the old-age pension comes. We take as an example a shoe laster from Leicester, who had worked thirty-seven years with one firm. 'When I heard the new manager going through and saying: "The whole of this side of this room, this room and this room is to be stopped," I knew it would be uphill work to get something.' He went on to describe to us how he had not been able to bring himself to tell his wife the bad news when he got home, how she had noticed that something was wrong, how confident she had been that he would get work elsewhere, but how he had known that the chances were heavily against him. For months and indeed often for years such men go on looking for work, and the same is true of many casual labourers.

Pilgrim Trust, *Men Without Work* (1938),
144–5

50 B. Abel-Smith and P. Townsend: The rediscovery of poverty, 1965

Abel-Smith and Townsend analysed the Ministry of Labour's family expenditure surveys of 1953–4 and 1960 to demonstrate the continuation of poverty in the welfare state. Notice how their indicators of poverty differ from those of Beveridge and Rowntree.

Two assumptions have governed much economic thinking in Britain since the war. The first is that we have 'abolished' poverty. The second is that we are a much more equal society – that the differences between the living standards of rich and poor are much smaller than they used to be.

These assumptions are of great practical as well as theoretical importance. They form the background to much of the discussion of social and economic policy. But are they true? . . .

Many attempts have been made to define 'poverty lines' for use in Britain in studies conducted in the past. . . . Rowntree was the first to attempt a really precise definition. He estimated the cost of buying the 'necessities' which he calculated were needed by different types of family to maintain physical efficiency. He then counted the families whose total income was insufficient to enable them to purchase these necessities. These were the families he described as living in poverty. In time his approach became widely accepted, first by social scientists and later by government. During the last war, when devising a new system of income security, Lord Beveridge recognized the advantages of this 'subsistence' standard and the government accepted his reasoning. . . .

We did not adopt this approach. . . . The principal measure of 'poverty' which we use in this paper is the level of living of National Assistance Board applicants in each year which is being studied. . . . Whatever may be said about the adequacy of the National Assistance Board level of living as a just or publicly approved measure of 'poverty', it has at least the advantage of being in a sense the 'official' operational definition of the minimum level of living at any particular time. . . . The approach which we have adopted follows from the principle that the minimum level of living regarded as acceptable by a society increases with rising national prosperity. . . .

In summary, in 1960 approximately 18 per cent of the households and 14·2 per cent of the persons in the United Kingdom, representing nearly 7,500,000 persons, were living below a defined 'national assistance' level of living. About 23 per cent were living in households primarily dependent on pensions, 23 per cent in households primarily dependent on other state benefits and 41 per cent in households primarily dependent on earnings. Many in this last group were members of large families. It seemed that there were about one million retired persons and half a million other persons not receiving national assistance, who were primarily dependent on state benefits and had a *prima facie* case which might have allowed them to qualify for supplementary help from the National Assistance Board. . . .

Finally, we conclude that the evidence of substantial numbers of the population living below national assistance level, and also of substantial numbers seeming to be eligible for national assistance but not receiving it, calls for a radical review of the whole social security scheme. Moreover, the fact that nearly a third of the poor were children suggests the need for a readjustment of priorities in plans for extensions and developments.

B. Abel-Smith and P. Townsend, *The Poor and the Poorest* (1965), 9–67

IV

The politics of welfare: parties and individuals

51 Joseph Chamberlain: Social legislation, 1885

Chamberlain's own peculiar Birmingham Bismarckianism is already evident in this early speech which contained the essence of the Radical programme of that year.

Social legislation . . . is not new. The Poor Law, for instance, is social legislation. It recognizes their right to live which *The Times* denies, and it is an endeavour on the part of the community to save themselves from the shame and disgrace of allowing any of their members to starve. Well, there are many people who propose to carry it farther. We shall hear in these times of depression, I imagine, a great deal about state-aided emigrants. For my own part I do not look on these proposals with much favour. I hope it may be possible to find work and employment for our own citizens at home without expatriating them against their will. The Education Act is a second instance of social legislation, and one of the most beneficent and useful. It is an endeavour to put in the hands of all an instrument wherewith alone advance in life becomes possible. But we have not gone far enough. We have made education compulsory, but we have omitted to make it free, and I hope that this great and necessary change will be one of the first to which reformers will direct their attention. On what ground do we levy a fee? Education is given because it is to the advantage of the children, but it is also to the advantage of the community, and the community ought to pay for it, and not the individual. We force the parents to give up the labour of his child at a time perhaps when it is almost necessary to the subsistence of the family. We ought not to go further and impose upon him a tax which is the most unfair tax that can be conceived, because it is a tax proportioned not to the ability of the man to pay, but to his necessities and wants. I cannot doubt that the example in this respect which has been set in the United States, in

Canada, in France, and almost throughout the Continent will soon be imitated in our own country.

L. Creswicke, *Life of Joseph Chamberlain*, 1 (n.d. 1904?), 172–4

52   Winston Churchill: Social reform, 1907

Churchill had a brief career as a social reformer in the Liberal governments of 1906–14. This extract sums up his approach to the issue.

Meanwhile another politician was showing interest in the field. Winston Churchill, on safari in Africa in the latter part of 1907, wrote to the editor of the *Westminster Review*: 'However willing the working classes may be to remain in passive opposition merely to the existing social system, they will not continue to bear, they cannot, the awful uncertainties of their lives. Minimum standards of wages and comfort, insurance in some effective form or other against sickness, unemployment, old age – these are the questions and the only questions by which parties are going to live in the future. . . . This is the sort of tune I think I will sing at Birmingham on the 23rd January: "Social bulwarks, security, standardization".'

H. Wilson Harris, *J. A. Spender* (1946), 81

53   David Lloyd George: Social reform – speech at Swansea, 1 October 1908

This is a classic presentation of the case for the approach of the new Liberalism to social reform.

The same observations apply to the question of civil equality. We have not yet attained to it in this country – far from it. You will not have established it in this land until the child of the poorest parent shall have the same opportunity for receiving the best education as the child of the richest.

British Liberalism is not going to repeat the errors of Continental Liberalism. The fate of Continental Liberalism should warn them of that danger. It has been swept on one side before it had well begun its work, because it refused to adapt itself to new conditions. The Liberalism of the Continent concerned itself exclusively with mending and perfecting the machinery which was to grind corn for the people. It forgot that the people had to live whilst the process was going on, and people saw their lives pass away without anything being accomplished. But British Liberalism has been better advised. It has not abandoned the traditional ambition of the Liberal Party to establish freedom and equality; but side by side with this effort it promotes measures for ameliorating the conditions of life for the multitude.

Poverty is the result of a man's own misconduct or misfortune. In so far as he brings it on himself, the state cannot accomplish much. It can do something, however, to protect him. In so far as poverty is due to circumstances over which the man has no control, then the state should step in to the very utmost limit of its resources, and save the man from the physical and mental torture involved in extreme penury.

Idleness is a more difficult problem, perhaps, than drinking, but much of this is also due to the lassitude and lack of vitality which comes from insufficient nourishment and bad conditions. Owing to these circumstances, men are not equipped with the necessary strength and energy for consistent and continuous toil. Better conditions of life for the people will produce an appreciable diminution in the numbers of the idle classes at both ends of the scale, for the state cannot well support both, and it must adopt the most effective method for getting rid of them. They are a burden and a source of danger. But there is another and a larger section of the poverty-stricken than these, and it is with that section I am mainly concerned – those who through no fault of their own are unable to earn their daily bread, the aged and infirm, the broken in health, the unemployed, and those dependent upon them. The aged we have dealt with during the present session. We are still confronted with the more gigantic task of dealing with the rest – the sick, the infirm, the unemployed, the widows, and the orphans. No country can lay any real claim to civilization that allows them to starve. Starvation is a punishment that society has ceased to inflict for centuries on its worst criminals, and at its most barbarous stage humanity never starved the children of the criminal.

I have heard some foolish mutterings that much recognition of this fact in legislation may drive capital away. There is nothing capital need fear as much as the despair of the multitude. And I should like to know whither it will flee, for, judging by the unmistakable symptoms of the times, there will soon be no civilized land in the world where proper provision for the aged, the broken, and the unfortunate amongst those who toil will not be regarded as the first charge upon the wealth of the land.

D. Lloyd George, Better Times (1910), 50–55

54   Labour: social reform, 1900

This manifesto of the Labour Representation Committee at the general election of 1900 reflects some of the optimism of the early labour movement that social reform could be achieved through political representation.

Adequate maintenance from national funds for the aged poor.
Public provision of better houses for the people.
Useful work for the unemployed.
Adequate maintenance for children.
No compulsory vaccination.
Public control of the liquor traffic.
Nationalization of land and railways.
Relief of local rates by grants from the national exchequer.
Legislative independence for all parts of the Empire.
Abolition of the standing army, and the establishment of a citizen force. The people to decide on peace or war.
Graduated income tax.
Shorter parliaments. Adult suffrage. Registration reform. Payment of members.

The object of these measures is to enable the people ultimately to obtain the socialization of the means of production, distribution, and exchange, to be controlled by a democratic state in the interests of the entire community, and the complete emancipation of labour from the domination of capitalism and landlordism, with the establishment of social and economic equality between the sexes.

> Manifesto of the Labour Representation
> Committee (1900), from F. W. S. Craig, *British
> General Election Manifestos, 1900–74* (1975), 3–4

55   The Archbishop of Canterbury: The redistribution of wealth, 1911

In this speech, Archbishop Lang shows the extent to which the rhetoric of the redistribution of wealth had become commonplace among the establishment by the eve of the first world war. Lang was a strong advocate of 'enlightened capitalism', according to his biographer.

The nineteenth century . . . was concerned with the creation of wealth: the twentieth century will be concerned with its distribution. There is none of us, whatever may be his political views, who does not feel that this is a problem which needs adjusting. We cannot but be appalled by the contrast of increasing prosperity and great wealth and of great poverty, of increasing luxury and of great squalor. . . . That contrast between the London of the west and the London I know so well of the east is a contrast which may be seen over the whole field of our English life. When I think of that great multitude of our working folk among whom I have laboured, whom I have learnt to reverence, I cannot but see the picture of the monotony of toil which they are called upon to bear, of the uncertainty of employment which haunts them day by day, of the overcrowded houses in which we ask and expect them to rear British homes, of the mean streets from which every sign not only of the beauty of God's earth but of the comforts and conveniences that are common to ours are shut out. . . . Our best self in the contemplation of this inequality says that these things ought not to be.

A. G. Lockhart, *Cosmo Gordon Lang* (1949), 239–40

56   The Labour Party: A national health service, 1918

This resolution indicates the extent to which the Labour Party in 1918 were already pointing the way towards a comprehensive national health service at the optimum standard possible.

That this conference declares that the organization and development of a unified health service for the whole community are questions of urgent importance, and that steps should be taken without delay to establish a Ministry of Health based upon public health services, and entirely dissassociated from any Poor Law taints.

(a) That to such a Ministry of Health should be transferred all the health services now coming under the Local Government Board, Board of Education, Home Office, Privy Council, National Health Insurance Commissions and Poor Law Acts.

(b) That a department for the care of infancy, maternity and old age, largely staffed by women, should be established, and increased powers be given to central and local authorities for work of this kind.

(c) That all duties relating to housing should be transferred to the new ministry, and that in this department also the services of women should be fully utilized.

(d) That there should be no representation of special interests, such as those of insurance societies, in the formation of such a ministry.

(e) That the public health committees of the local authorities, with such further provision as is necessary in view of their increased duties on the lines of the composition of the education committees, should be the centres of local administration.

(f)   That the Public Health Acts should be extended so as to include within their scope all those duties now so inadequately provided under the Poor Law, and all further services that are necessary to secure and maintain the health of the community.

Labour Party, *Annual Conference Report* (1918),
124–5

57   The origins of the Beveridge Report, 1941

The document records a deputation by the general council of the Trades Union Congress to the Minister of Health and the Secretary of State for Scotland in February 1941, which led to the setting up of the Beveridge Committee. Notice the apparently circumscribed terms of references of the committee.

The general council of the Trades Union Congress receive continual representations from affiliated organizations about national health insurance. It is pointed out that the amount of cash benefit provided under the scheme is far below unemployment insurance, unemployment assistance, public assistance, pensions, workmen's compensation or the provisions of the personal injuries (civilians) scheme.

People cannot understand why national health insurance benefit, for which they have paid contributions, should not be paid to them when they are ill if the cause of their illness happens to bring them payments under the Workmen's Compensation Acts. Indeed the matter goes further, because if a person is entitled to workmen's compensation, even though he may not actually receive it, he can still be deprived of national health insurance benefit.

Then again, national health insurance provides no benefit whatever for dependants whilst all the other schemes referred to above do.

We are definitely of the opinion that the country cannot continue to afford the inefficient and incomplete services rendered to insured persons together with the expensive muddle and waste associated with it.

We, therefore, ask the ministry of health to take the lead in an examination of the whole position with a view to plans being produced at an early date which would provide a properly balanced scheme for the insured person.

The question of paying for it has of course to be faced, but we feel sure that neither the insured person nor anybody else will object to paying, provided they know that their money is not being wasted.

It may be said that the present time is not opportune for examination of this kind, but on the other hand it is essential that plans for the future should be ready at the earliest possible moment, firstly, because there must be better provision for people when peace comes again and, secondly, because the nation cannot afford to allow inefficiency and waste, therefore, coordinated planning should be put in operation.

As a result of that deputation the Minister of Health announced in the House of Commons on the 22 May 1941 that the government were setting up an interdepartmental committee with the following terms of reference:

'To undertake, with special reference to the interrelation of the schemes, a survey of the existing national schemes of social insurance and allied services, including workmen's compensation, and to make recommendations.'

> Memoranda from Organizations, Social Insurance and Allied Services, Cmnd. 6405 (1942), 13–15

58   Winston Churchill: Reception of the Beveridge Report, 1943

These extracts, from two notes circulated to the Cabinet early in 1943, bring out Churchill's lukewarm, though constitutionally correct, attitude to the report.

1   A dangerous optimism is growing up about the conditions it will be possible to establish here after the war. Unemployment and low wages are to be abolished, education greatly improved and prolonged; great developments in housing and health will be undertaken; agriculture is to be maintained at least at its new high level. At the same time the cost of living is not to be raised. The Beveridge plan of social insurance, or something like it, is to abolish want. The money which the wage-earning class have saved during the war in nest-eggs or accumulated by war savings certificates must not lose its value.

2   Our foreign investments have almost disappeared. The United States will be a strong competitor with British shipping. We shall have great difficulties in placing our necessary exports profitably. Meanwhile, in order to help Europe, we are to subject ourselves to a

prolonged period of rationing and distribute a large part of our existing stocks. We are to develop the tropical colonies and raise the condition of their inhabitants. We must clearly keep a large air force and navy, so as not to be set upon again by the Germans, and large military forces will be needed to garrison the enemy countries and make sure they do not begin again to rearm for revenge.

3   The question steals across the mind whether we are not committing our forty-five million people to tasks beyond their compass, and laying on them burdens beyond their capacity to bear. While not disheartening our people by dwelling on the dark side of things, ministers should, in my view, be careful not to raise false hopes, as was done last time by speeches about 'homes for heroes', etc. The broad mass of the people face the hardships of life undaunted, but they are liable to get very angry if they feel they have been gulled or cheated. . . .

I think we should handle this matter in the following way, which I gather from the reports I have seen is very much what my colleagues desire.

1   This approach to social security, bringing the magic of averages nearer to the rescue of the millions, constitutes an essential part of any post-war scheme of national betterment.

2   There may be portions of it which would probably not be found workable or acceptable. It is desirable, however, that should the measure be produced it should be an integral conception and not merely what is left after the critics have pulled out certain weak points.

3   There should be a body – if necessary a commission – set up to work from now till the end of the war, polishing, reshaping, and preparing for the necessary legislation.

4   We cannot, however, initiate the legislation now or commit ourselves to the expenditure involved. That can only be done by a responsible government and a House of Commons refreshed by contact with the people. We do not know what conditions will be at the end of the war, or how the expenditure on social insurance will fit in with other social expenditure desired, or how this group of betterment expenditure can be reconciled with the need for maintaining strong naval and air forces and a certain military force for a considerable time. We do not know what government is going to be in power after the war, or what prime minister. We should get everything ready for

them, and leave them a free hand to take up or reject a scheme which
will be perfected in itself.

> W. S. Churchill, Cabinet notes (12 January
> and 14 February 1943), from W. S. Churchill,
> *The Second World War* IV, *The Hinge of Fate*
> (1951), 861–2

59   R. A. Butler: The Education Act of 1944

Butler used the lull in party and sectarian conflict over education during the
second world war to bring in a major education bill. Here he outlines the
problems, the tactics and the support.

Shortly after assuming office I told the House of Commons that it was
necessary to reform the law relating to education, and a few weeks later
I sent the Prime Minister a letter stressing the need to adapt the
educational system to present social requirements. I instanced the
need for industrial and technical training and for a settlement with the
churches about their schools and about religious instruction in
schools. This was on 12 September 1941. The next day the Prime
Minister replied as follows: 'It would be a great mistake to raise the
1902 controversy during the war, and I certainly cannot contemplate a
new education bill. I think it would also be a great mistake to stir up
the public schools question at the present time. No one can possibly
tell what the financial and economic state of the country will be when
the war is over.' . . .

In March 1943 . . . I was invited to spend the night at Chequers. . . .
He [the Prime Minster] read four pages on education, which were in a
flowing style and derived from Disraeli's view that a nation rules either
by force or tradition. His theme was that we must adhere to our
traditions, but that we must move from the class basis of our politics,
economics and education to a national standard. There were some
sharp words about idle people whether at the top or the bottom, some
very pungent remarks about the old school tie (the time for which, he
said, was past), and a definite assertion that the school leaving age must
be raised to 16. . . .

The sequel to my visit was . . . a memorandum on educational
reconstruction to the Cabinet; in July I published the white paper,

decorated by a quotation from Disraeli ('Upon the education of the people of this country the fate of this country depends'), and in January 1944 I moved the second reading of the Education Bill. . . . The reception of the white paper made it plain to my ministerial colleagues that, whilst there might be controversy over certain sections of the bill, and particularly over the religious settlement, it would have the minimum of disruptive effect upon the coalition character of the government. . . .

It may seem strange that the enormous capital and current commitments which the full implementation of the Education Bill would entail were not considered an insuperable barrier to progress. But I was very careful at all stages to say, what was indeed the case, that their full implementation would take at least a generation. . . . I was also encouraged by the whips' office . . . for whom the beauty of the bill was that it would keep the parliamentary troops thoroughly occupied; providing endless opportunity for debate, without any fear of breaking up the government. Its provisions were broadly acceptable to moderate and progressive Conservative opinion and consistently supported by Labour men, both those inside the government (notably Ernest Bevin) and those 'in opposition' (notably our former colleague Arthur Greenwood).

R. A. Butler, *The Art of the Possible* (1973 edn),
95–118

60   The Labour Party: Public and private pensions, 1963

This document illustrates the relationship between occupational pensions schemes and state flat-rate pensions. The Labour Party proposals show the extent to which it accepted the need for redistribution and the limits on that redistribution.

While national insurance benefits have been lagging behind inadequate national assistance scales, the government has encouraged employers to develop their own private insurance schemes, and helped their financing by a lavish policy of tax concessions. In the case of old-age pensions, preparation of schemes for private employers has developed into a profitable field of operation for many insurance companies, and the trustees of the huge funds, at present being built up by thousands of private superannuation schemes, are now becoming one of the largest group of investors in the City of London. But only half the employed population are members of these schemes, and the pensions they receive are usually small. Only a small minority draw really worthwhile pensions or have their wages fully made up by their employers when they are sick.

We are in no way opposed to the provision by progressive employers – whether private or public – of their own superannuation, redundancy and sickness schemes. Indeed, we regard such provision as a useful addition to any really adequate state system. What we want to emphasize, however, is that outside the public services, the nationalized industries and a few progressive firms, this kind of private social security is normally linked to a minority of executives, white-collar employees and industrial workers on the staff. Many millions of working people today still belong to the other nation.

Faced by this problem of the two nations, what has the government done? Instead of trying to narrow the gap, it has widened the gap. By combining a low level of national insurance benefit with generous tax concessions, it has almost compelled the employer with a conscience to establish his own private system of privileged social security. By shifting more and more of the burden of social security from the taxpayer to the national insurance contributor, it has made an unfair system of flat rate contributions bear ever more harshly on the lower-paid worker. Finally, by introducing its own so-called graded pension scheme, it has created yet another ingenious device for making the national insurance contributor pay an even larger share of the cost of social security – in return for ludicrously inadequate benefits.

One result of these policies has been to undermine the insurance principle, and to turn what – when it began – was a genuine insurance scheme, into an intolerably complicated system of discriminating taxation. Another result has been a bureaucratic nightmare of such complexity that the average contributor is quite unable to sort it out. From the government's point of view, however, this complexity has the advantage that it conceals the success with which the cost of social security has been transferred from the wealthier taxpayer and the employer, and is now almost exclusively borne by the national insurance contributor.

This is the essence of Labour's new plan. Its three aims are:

1   To restore the comprehensive character of national insurance and to provide subsistence benefits as of right and without recourse to the National Assistance Board.

2   On this foundation of subsistence, to build a new structure of graded benefits related to individual earnings and individual needs.

3   To finance the improved benefits by substituting wage-related for flat rate contributions.

The Labour Party, *New Frontiers for Social Security* (1963)

61   Richard Crossman: The politics of national health, 1972

Here Crossman deals with the difficulty in reconciling the principle of medical freedom and no state interference, on the one hand, and state financing on the other.

If you take the consultants in the teaching hospitals, there is a different guarantee of freedom which enables them to combine private practice with salaried work for a board of governors or regional hospital board. Now those were the two principles which had to be fused successfully and they were fused by Aneurin Bevan in a hurried compromise which he himself regarded as very unsatisfactory and which was the result of negotiated deals designed to split the medical profession in such a way that he could get the service into operation. In order to break the opposition of the BMA, broadly representing the general practitioners, he bought out the consultants. They were permitted a very remarkable relationship under which they were to be appointed to be National Health Service consultants and if they wished, they were going to be able to have so many elevenths of their time (I've never quite understood how each one calculates his elevenths – but this is the system, this was the deal) which they could take away from the Health Service and allocate to private practice. In addition they were given merit awards to compensate them for the loss of private practice. Mr Bevan gave them a firm and extremely power-ful position, a position which they have developed steadily ever since.

One of the things I discovered by being various kinds of minster is the operation of various kinds of pressure groups in various kinds of politics. The doctors' politics are similar in certain ways to the politics of the NFU. The farmers are stratified very similarly to the doctors, and they too have a passion for individualism, and for political infighting. It would surprise many people to realize what passion solid farmers and sensible doctors can 'whip up' in their hearts when they face the dangers of Whitehall and Westminster. There is a common tradition of suspicion and though both have been very largely dependent on the largesse of Westminster and Whitehall for their standard of living, they have combined the willingness to receive the state's money with the gravest suspicion of the motives of those who provide it.

There is also an interesting resemblance between the structure of the BMA and the structure of the National Farmers Union. Both are led and dominated by the outstanding and powerful men in the profession who have to speak as advocates for men less powerful than themselves and don't do too badly out of it at the same time. Any Minister of Health and Social Security has to spend a very large amount of his time in medical politics, and one soon discovers that within the BMA there is not complete unity of view any more than there is between the East Anglian 'barley barons' and the Scottish sheep farmers. If I dare to say it here in this distinguished company, I found that, for instance, the clash between the junior hospital doctors and the senior consultants was nearly as passionate as that between all of them and me. With the GPs over here and the junior hospital doctors over there and the senior consultants at the top, there was tremendous politicking between them. But they all presented a united front against me. And because I farm at home, I felt wholly at home in dealing with the BMA.

R. H. S. Crossman, *A Politician's View of Health Service Planning* (Glasgow 1972), 8–9

62   The Labour Party: Social justice, 1974

This extract from the Labour Party manifesto for the February general election in 1974 should be compared with documents 54, 56 and 60.

Social justice
Clearly, a fresh approach to the British crisis is required, and Labour insists that it must begin with an entirely new recognition of the claims of social justice.

To that end, urgent action is needed to tackle rising prices; to strike at the roots of the worst poverty; to make the country demonstrably a much fairer place to live in. For these purposes, a new Labour government, in its first period of office, will:

1   Bring immediate help to existing *pensioners*, widows, the sick and the unemployed by increasing pensions and other benefits to £10 for the single person and £16 for the married couple, within the first parliamentary session of our government. Thereafter these figures will be increased annually in proportion to increases in average national earnings. We shall also follow this by replacing the Conservative government's inadequate and unjust long-term pensions scheme by a

comprehensive scheme designed to take future pensioners off the means test and give full equality of treatment to women.

2   Introduce a new scheme of help for the *disabled*.

3   Help the low-paid and other families in povery by introducing a new system of *child cash allowances* for every child, including the first, payable to the mother.

4   Introduce strict *price control* on key services and commodities.

6   *Redistribute income and wealth.* We shall introduce an annual wealth tax on the rich; bring in a new tax on major transfers of personal wealth; heavily tax speculation in property – including a new tax on property companies; and seek to eliminate tax dodging across the whole field.

Labour Party, *Let Us Work Together – Labour's Way out of the Crisis* (1974), 7–9

63   The social wage and public expenditure cuts, 1975

This is a left-wing analysis of the cuts in social services in the context of the 'Social Contract'.

When it comes to cuts in the social wage will all these areas be cut equally? An important part of the government's argument is that the country must use this time of hardship and general belt-tightening to get fit for the boom to come; that money must be diverted to encourage industry to invest in new plant and equipment to be ready for the future upturn in world trade. As the *Observer* argued (August 1975) 'Ultimately, money can really be found for industry only if is taken from someone else: and since even Chancellor Healey now appears to agree that the British are taxed up to the hilt this can only come from cuts in public spending.'

The sequence of events – the introduction of wage controls preceding social spending cuts – is not without its own significance. It goes some way towards explaining the apparent contradiction between the current rise in public expenditure and the simultaneous news of cuts. It also suggests that there are likely to be much more devastating cuts to come. For the Labour government has managed to impose an incomes policy far harsher than that which brought down the Heath government in 1974. It has done so on the strength of a socialist rhetoric: by being 'the party of the people' for social equality etc. For that government to be seen to be attacking the welfare state at the same time as it was winning official union backing for pay cuts, probably only previously matched by those of the 30s, was clearly impossible. So, the wage cuts came first.

Counter Information Services, Special Report, *Cutting the Welfare State (Who Profits?)* (1975), 4

V

Welfare in practice: the administration of social legislation

64 Walter Long: The appointment of the Royal Commission on the Poor Laws, 1904

Long was Conservative president of the Local Government Board and here he outlines the need to have an inquiry into the Poor Laws to head off radical demands.

The Prime Minister,

I am very strongly of the opinion, and have been for some time, that there is every justification for a fresh inquiry – indeed I have more than once suggested that something of the sort was inevitable, but I trust I may be allowed to express my strong hope that no encouragement of any kind should be given to Mr Samuel.

I happen to know that the Radicals are trying to get credit both for what we do and for what must be the logical outcome of our policy. . . .

I have been for some time collecting material in order to lay a memorandum before you and I will put it into shape at once if you so desire.

Would it please you to answer Mr Samuel somewhat to the following effect – 'That the suggestion is one for which there is much to be said and that the government have had it under consideration for some little time, but that the present moment is not opportune for any pronouncement.'

I hope I have not presumed too far in making these suggestions but I see so much here of the machinations of the Radicals and Socialists that I am naturally anxious they should not get credit for what they do not deserve, and that nothing should be done to distract public attention from that which is immediately necessary, viz, the active prosecution and development of the scheme I have laid before the public. It is of course obvious that the experience gained by these central committees must be of material assistance to us in deciding what form an inquiry should take.

From J. Brown, 'The Appointment of the 1905 Poor Law Commission', *Bulletin of the Institute of Historical Research* 39 (1969), 240

65   The administration of national health insurance, 1913

The quantification of the extent and nature of sickness among women was one of the results of the National Insurance Act of 1911.

No reliable information as to the sickness prevalent among women existed before the act came into operation. The returns of expenditure on benefits for the first year of the act, when analysed and tabulated, will supply the first collection of useful data as to the sickness risks of women; and even this experience will have to be adjusted to secure the elimination of figures representing unjustifiable claims before it can be regarded as statistically valuable. The rate of sickness provided for in the case of women was, in these circumstances, practically the same as in the case of men. If it be admitted that, other things being equal, women are subject to a greater amount of sickness than men, it must be borne in mind that occupational conditions do not increase the average rate of sickness among all insured women to the same extent as in the case of insured men; and that in the common rate of sickness employed for the purposes of the act the natural excess in the case of women may be deemed to be represented by the occupational excess provided for in the case of men. If due weight be given to this consideration as well as to the fact that the real extent of sickness among women was unknown, it will be agreed, doubtless, that difficulty would have been experienced in coming to the conclusion in 1911 that women ought to pay for sickness insurance at a relatively higher rate than was required of men.

Future provision
(i)   Sickness among married women
So much being said in support of the considerations which dictated the original rates of contribution, it seems evident that some revision of the finance of the act in respect of women will be necessary. A substantial part of the excess of claims which has been revealed is due to the claims of women (almost entirely, of course, married women), in respect of the period of pregnancy. Many of these claims, doubtless,

have been on the border line of justification. Nearly all of them represent demands which were unknown to the relatively few friendly societies of women which existed before the act, and which, if not explicitly precluded by the rules, would still in general have been repudiated by those societies as inconsistent with insurance against sickness.

(ii) Sickness among women generally

Apart from this difficulty, there are indications that, despite the relatively high rate of sickness provided for, the contributions are insufficient in the case of women generally. A remedy for this insufficiency could be found in a moderate alteration of the statutory apportionment of the contributions of women between the societies and the sinking fund.

> Report for 1913–14 on the Administration of
> National Health Insurance, Cd. 7496 (1914),
> 60–61

66   (see opposite)

67   'The Geddes Axe', 1922

The Committee on National Expenditure chaired by Sir Eric Geddes, composed entirely of businessmen and financiers, was set up to recommend cuts in public expenditure.

Terms of reference

To make recommendations to the Chancellor of the Exchequer for effecting forthwith all possible reductions in the national expenditure on supply services, having regard especially to the present and prospective position of the revenue. In so far as questions of policy are involved in the expenditure under discussion, these will remain for the exclusive consideration of the Cabinet; but it will be open to the committee to review the expenditure and to indicate the economies which might be effected if particular policies were either adopted, abandoned or modified. . . .

Introduction to the report on government expenditure on social services, namely, education, health, labour and old-age pensions

The provisional estimates submitted to the committee of the cost of these services in 1922/23 in Great Britain amount to over £124,000,000, being nearly four times the pre-war expenditure.

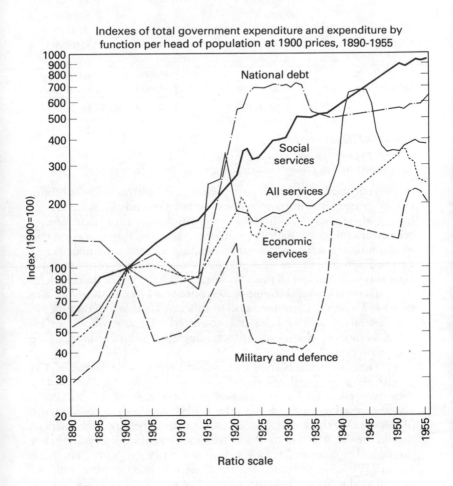

Indexes of total government expenditure and expenditure by function per head of population at 1900 prices, 1890-1955

Note the steady rate of growth of social services expenditure in real terms per head of population compared with other elements of government spending.

A. T. Peacock and J. V. Wiseman, *The Growth of Public Expenditure in the United Kingdom* (1961), 87

	1913/14 Audited expenditure £	1921/22 Estimate £	1922/23 Provisional estimate £
Education	17,200,000	60,500,000	59,300,000
Health	5,000,000	29,000,000	27,900,000
Labour	900,000	21,500,000	14,500,000
Old-age pensions	9,800,000	21,700,000	22,300,000
	32,900,000	132,700,000	124,000,000

Ministry of Health estimates
Summary of conclusions
As a result of our consideration, we are of the opinion:

1   That both in policy and where administrative possibilities existed, successful efforts to economize have recently been made. We have indicated a few directions in which we think that further economies might be made. The principal items of this vote appertain to the housing schemes, which is entailing a cost to the taxpayer of £10,000,000 a year for the next 60 years, and we recommend a vigorous policy of sale of these houses in order to reduce that burden.

2   That no financial incentive to economy is given to those who are entrusted with the administration of this vast property. Economies in administration and upkeep are entrusted to those who have no financial interest whatsoever in decreasing the loss on the undertaking they manage.

3   That as regards national health insurance, the state has progressively accepted additional burdens and additional costs when they occurred, and has not reaped any benefit from the 'windfalls' which accrued to the funds of the approved societies as a consequence of the war. We think that, as soon as opportunity offers, such burdens should be transferred to the insurance organizations, where they might well be compensated for, in part at any rate, by betterment in the actuarial position and that a very small increase in contribution should be imposed to meet the additional cost of medical and other benefits now borne by the state in excess of its proper share of two ninths.

4   That as regards public health services, e.g. tuberculosis, maternity and child welfare, there can be no question as to the merits of the objects to be attained. There has, however, been a very large increase in this form of public expenditure since 1918/19, and, while we do not recommend reductions in this expenditure, we do feel that,

having regard to the present financial position, the state's contribution next year, at any rate, should not be above the figure provided for the current year. The contribution should be on a lump-sum basis, and not on a percentage basis. We hope that, with falling prices and the greatly increased incentive to economy, the authorities responsible for this form of activity will be able still further to increase their beneficial work.

Labour

1   That so long as unemployment insurance is on the present basis, employment exchanges are required as agencies for checking payments of unemployment insurance benefits, not as labour exchanges.

2   That the present unemployment insurance scheme is only partially a mutual insurance scheme, and is very complicated and costly to administer on that account.

3   That a committee of experts should be set up forthwith, with a view to simplifying the unemployment insurance scheme, amalgamating unemployment and health insurance cards, records, and, as far as possible, administration, and exploring the possibility of developing unemployment insurance by industry.

4   That the scope of the Industrial Relations Department should be considered as also the work of the Trade Boards Division after receipt of the report of Lord Cave's committee, and that their transfer to the Board of Trade should also be considered.

5   That subject to (3) and (4) the abolition of the employment exchanges and of the Ministry of Labour should be considered.

6   That as regards services arising out of the war, which are rapidly drawing to a close, there are directions where economies representing some £500,000 might be effected.

7   That owing to the uncertainty which prevails at the present time and the direct bearing on this estimate of the rate of unemployment, the sum available for 1922/23 cannot be reduced below the amount shown in the preliminary estimates.

> First Interim Report of the Committee on
> National Expenditure, Cmd. 1581 (1922),
> 2–148

68   The May Committee: The reduction of public expenditure, 1931

The May Committee was set up to advise the Labour government on cuts in public expenditure since the House of Commons considered that the burden of taxation was restricting industry and employment.

Factors, political and economic, in the present situation

Reviewing the course of national finance since the war, one cannot fail to notice how unequal is the continual struggle between expansion and retrenchment. One government, one parliament can embark on schemes which for all practical purposes definitely commit future governments, future parliaments as far ahead as one can look. With some schemes not only are the main lines permanent, but so strong are the contractual or moral obligations involved that any modification in the direction of economy is a difficult matter. But no government or parliament can bind its successors to economies. A few Cabinet decisions, a few votes of parliament, and all the savings achieved with much labour over a period of years may easily be dissipated.

So heavily loaded are the dice in favour of expenditure that no representation we can make is more important than to emphasize the need for caution in undertaking any commitments of a continuing character. This need has long been recognized in the national machinery of financial control – in the admirable standing order of the House of Commons that it will not 'proceed upon any motion for a grant or charge upon the public revenue . . . unless recommended from the crown'; in the pre-eminence of the Treasury among departments; in the method of preparation and presentation of estimates and in the checks on the levying of new taxation; but we must regretfully admit that – particularly since the war – this machinery has been lamentably neutralized by circumstances outside its control.

The cause is not far to seek. After the heavy sacrifices of the war, large sections of the nation looked to the post-war period with the natural expectation of a general improvement in the old conditions of life. The disappointment of many hopes in the economic sphere seemed to intensify demands for improvements from political action and all parties have felt the insistent pressure for promises of 'reforms' as the price of support, such 'reforms' being in fact mostly of the nature of privileges or benefits for particular classes at the cost of the general taxpayer. The results of this pressure are to be seen not only in the lavish promises contained in the election addresses of the period since the war but in the undertakings freely given by individual parliamentary candidates to sections of the electorate. At election times those desiring increased expenditure on particular objects are usually far better organized, far more active and vocal than those who favour the vague and uninspiring course of strict economy; and as a result candidates not infrequently find themselves returned to parliament committed, on a one-sided presentation of a case, to a course which on fuller knowledge they see to be opposed to the national interests. Especially serious is this danger at the present time when the mass of the electorate still does not appreciate the true economic position of the country and its problems. . . .

Social services
The general review given in our opening chapter of the increase of government expenditure since 1924 showed that of the total increases on various heads likely to reach about £130,000,000 this year, about £80,000,000 could be ascribed to developments of social services, including both those administered by the government and those under the direct control of local authorities. As regards the latter class, the state contribution represents only a part of the cost and for a complete picture it would be necessary to look also at the accounts of local authorities. Indeed, as regards some social services a large part is played also by private effort. . . .

Thus between 1911 and 1929 the total cost of these services grew to more than five times its former figure, the charge on rates was trebled, and the charge on the Exchequer was multiplied four and a half times. It is, however, satisfactory to note how very great has been the extension in this period of the policy of requiring contributions towards the cost of social services from those who benefit from them, directly or indirectly.

Since 1929 there has been a further increase of roughly £70,000,000 in the gross cost of unemployment insurance and a steady growth of most of the other items in the table, and it is roughly correct to say that the above services in the current year are costing the country in one form or another about seven times what they cost in 1911. An increase of this charge on the country's productive capacity would have been a serious matter, notwithstanding the change in the value of money, had our trade continued to develop as in the years immediately prior to the war. Under the difficult conditions of the post-war period, the increase of burden has been a grave handicap, and we cannot shut our eyes to the fact that the enormous increase in the Exchequer charge for these services has been the prime cause of the present crisis in the national finances.

Had it been possible to make sufficient reductions in other fields of expenditure we would gladly have been content with comparatively minor adjustments in this field. No such alternative is open and we cannot escape the conclusion that, under existing conditions and bearing in mind the rapid downward tendency in the price level with its inevitable reactions on the cost of living and wages, the rapid growth of this expenditure should be stopped and a large reduction made in the existing charge on the Exchequer.

Committee on National Expenditure Report,
Cmd. 3920 (1931), 12–13, 142, 145

69   The administration of the 'genuinely seeking work' clause of the Unemployment Insurance Act of 1921

The umpire's decision reveals the extent of discretion open to civil servants in the administration of this clause and some of the criteria to be applied to those claiming unemployment benefit.

In considering whether a person is genuinely seeking work the most important fact to be ascertained is the state of the applicant's mind. If a person genuinely wants work, that is, really prefers working for wages to living on benefits, it is probable that she is genuinely seeking it. But if a person prefers benefit to wages, or is content to be without work so long as she receives benefit, it may be presumed that she is not genuinely seeking it. Action is guided by desire, and whilst few people genuinely seek what they do not desire, most people genuinely seek what they really desire.

The genuineness of an applicant's desire for work must be considered in the light of all the circumstances available. Her record of employment is most important. If an applicant has been for many years a steady worker, and there has been no change in her circumstances, which relieves her of the necessity of working, the inference that she wants work is very strong. Her present needs, the amount which she can earn when at work as compared with the amount of benefit which she would receive, and the circumstances in which she lost her last employment, are all matters for consideration, though it would not be fair to assume that a person does not desire work, and is not genuinely seeking work, merely because she can live in resonable comfort without it or because she is as well off when on benefit as when at work.

As to the present applicants, their record of work, their present needs, the high rate of wages they got when at work as compared with the amount they would receive as benefit, and the circumstances in which they left their last employment, all indicate that they desire work and probably prefer it to idleness.

But though it may be probable that a person who wants work is genuinely seeking work, it is not necessarily so, and an applicant who is genuinely seeking work should generally be able to show that besides registering for work at an exchange she is making personal efforts on her own behalf to find work and is not content merely to wait till it is thrust on her.

Umpire's decision 1404/26 (14 July 1926)
from A. Deacon, *In Search of the Scrounger*
(1976), 95

70   E. W. Bakke: The administration of unemployment insurance, 1933

Bakke, by participant observation and interviewing, tried to capture what it was like to face a court of referees under the Unemployment Insurance Act which tested the 'genuineness' of the applicant's search for work.

I doubt very much whether a court, no matter how carefully chosen and how thoroughly respected, can apply fairly and adequately tests which will show the genuineness of a person's unemployment or industrial status, if it is not possible to formulate contribution or automatic employment-record tests which will determine that fact. The determination of industrial status, or the 'genuineness' of the unemployment before a court of referees is surrounded by many and perhaps insurmountable difficulties.

The attitude of the person involved as he approaches the court of referees is the first obstacle. Let us suppose for a moment that we have a court which is fair-minded and anxious to deal justly with its case. What sort of a human problem are they dealing with? First of all, he is a person who has in all probability been out of work for some time. If he is before the court as a 'not normally' case he has been out of work for at least 74 weeks out of the last 104. In the last two years he has not had thirty weeks of either full-time or part-time employment. The effects of this idleness have been discussed elsewhere. The person is 'down in the mouth' or 'fed up' or feels 'all washed out' or he can be described by any one of the dozen such descriptive terms which unemployed workers apply to their own condition. For two years he has tried day after day to find a place in a working world and failed. He is beginning to wonder if he will ever be needed again. Every week out of work finds the task more impossible. Every week increases the number of competitors between him and the job. He may be more skilled even after a long rest than the man just off the job. In his heart he often believes he is. But how is the employer to know this? He cannot test a number of men and take the best. He needs a man this morning, and the two rough and ready tests are, 'have you a reference', and 'how long have you been out?'

This man before the court knows this. He knows his chances of getting back at the old job are getting fewer and fewer. The alternatives he faces are two. He can 'take anything', and thus journey farther away from his trade, or he can hold out a little longer. Sometimes the first alternative isn't very real. There may be very little of 'anything' to do.

E. W. Bakke, *The Unemployed Man* (1933), 102–3

71 The administration of unemployment insurance: financial considerations, 1934

The Unemployment Insurance Statutory Committee was set up under the Unemployment Insurance Act of 1934 following strong pressure from employers, among others. They wanted a body to control and restrict expenditure on social services, though in practice this one was limited to unemployment insurance and to an advisory role.

Reference and procedure
By Section 17 (2) of the Unemployment Insurance Act, 1934, we are required, not later than the end of February in every year, to report on the financial condition of the unemployment fund on the 31st December last preceding. We may make a report on the financial condition of the fund at such other times as we think fit and we are required to make a report, whenever we consider that the fund is or is likely to become, and is likely to continue to be insufficient to discharge its liabilities. If, in making any report, we conclude that the fund is or is likely to become, and is likely to continue to be insufficient to discharge its liabilities, or is and is likely to continue to be more than reasonably sufficient to discharge its liabilities, then, by Section 17 (3) of the act, we are required to recommend such changes in the rates of contribution or in the rates or conditions of benefit as, in our opinion, are required to make the fund sufficient or not more than reasonably sufficient to discharge its liabilities.

By Section 17 (4) of the act, we are required to give such notice as we think sufficient of our intention to make a report on the financial condition of the fund, and to take into consideration any representations made to us with respect thereto. We gave notice, accordingly, on 18th January 1935, by publication in the press and otherwise, of our intention to make a report by the end of February and we asked that any representations should be sent to us on or before 14th February. In response, we received written representations from the National Confederation of Employers' Organizations, from the Trades Union Congress general council, from the 'Children's Minimum Organizing Committee', and from the standing joint committee of Industrial Women's Organizations. Representatives of the second and third of these bodies appeared before us at our meeting on the 7th February.

The National Confederation of Employers' Organizations urged that the first charge on any disposable surplus of the unemployment fund should be a reduction of contributions. The Trades Union Congress general council advocated several minor changes, affecting the statutory conditions for benefit and dependants' allowances, which they had previously laid before the Royal Commission on Unemployment Insurance; they put forward also suggestions for increase of children's allowances and for grant of benefit in their own right to boys and girls between 14 and 16. The 'Children's Minimum Organizing Committee' advocated an increase of children's allowances, having regard both to estimates of physical needs and to the published scales of assistance under the Unemployment Assistance Board. The standing joint committee of Industrial Women's Organizations advocated increases in the rates of benefit for women contributors, and for dependent children, and proposed that children between 14 and 16 who satisfy the first statutory condition should be entitled to benefit in their own right.

> Unemployment Insurance Statutory Committee, First Report, House of Commons 49 (1935), 2

72   The case for selective benefits and greater reliance on the market in the provision of welfare, 1967

We begin with assumptions and general propositions concerning the present conditions and probable trends in economic society.

(a) Real incomes are rising and, after addition of state benefits and deduction of taxes, are becoming less unequal. Economic and social advance make possible (i) more generous aid for people with low incomes, (ii) more choice for people with rising incomes, (iii) more total expenditure on welfare than is being or can be financed collectively by taxation.

(b) The number of people remaining in need before allowing for state aid varies with the definition of 'poverty' (or 'deprivation' or 'the submerged'). If it is defined in *absolute* terms of the amount of food, clothing and shelter required for subsistence it is a diminishing quantity. If it is defined in *relative* terms as the proportion between low incomes and average incomes it can be a diminishing, unchanging or growing quantity, but it is then a measure of the *distribution* of income rather than of poverty in the absolute sense of deprivation of the materials required for tolerable existence. In this relative sense 'poverty' loses some of its readily acceptable, common-sense meaning, since it can remain and even intensify as incomes rise in all parts of a society becoming more wealthy.

(c) State aid in Britain should be such that poverty in the absolute sense has been abolished. Remaining poverty can then come only from refusal or ignorance of state aid.

(d) State aid in cash may be necessary but aid in kind should be the final resort after

(i) encouragement to families, or at least removal of obstacles, to circulate income between its better-off and worse-off members;
(ii) encouragement for voluntary aid.

(e) If poverty in the absolute sense is to be abolished by state aid, it must be measured in terms of individual needs and means, and individual aid must be varied accordingly. The matching of aid to individual needs and means requires a measure or test of means and needs. Reluctance to match aid to individual circumstances, based largely on recollection of the household means test in the 1930s, is a barrier to more generous and more humane aid to the remaining needy.

(f) Generous and humane aid is hindered by the continuance of equal social benefits irrespective of individual circumstances, as in the provision of free or subsidized education, health services, housing, pensions and other state services.

> Institute of Economic Affairs, *Towards a*
> *Welfare Society* (1967), 13–14

73   R. M. Titmuss: The case against selectivity in social welfare, 1968

How to include poor people, and especially poor coloured people, in our societies, and at the same time to channel proportionately more resources in their favour without inducing shame or stigma, remains one of the great challenges for social policy in Britain and the USA. The answers will not be found by creating separate apartheid-like structures and 'public burden' services for poor people; nor will they be found through short-term 'gimmicks' and slogans or by expecting the computer to solve the problems which human beings have not yet adequately diagnosed.

Those in Britain who are now muddled about the current debate, headlined as 'universalism versus selectivity', should study American experience. They are muddled because of the mixture of ideas in the apparently simple cries: 'Let us concentrate help on those whose needs are greatest'; 'Why provide benefits for those who do not really need them?'

Many people are muddled because there is a case for more selective services and benefits provided, as social rights, on the basis of the needs of certain categories, groups and territorial areas (e.g. Plowden's 'educational priority areas') and not on the basis of individual means; there is a problem (as there always has been) of priorities in the allocation of scarce resources in the social policy field; there is a case for more redistribution through taxing the middle and upper-middle classes more heavily by making them pay higher contributions for, e.g., medical care and higher education; there is a problem of finding more money for social security, education, health, the welfare services, housing, roads, and all sectors of all the public services.

'Selectivity' can mean many different things (which is rarely understood) but to most critics of 'welfare statism' is denotes an individual means test – some inquiry into resources to identify poor people who should be provided with free services or cash benefits, be excused charges or pay lower charges. . . .

The purpose of this article was not, however, to discuss the financing of the social services or the reform of taxation. I have tried to be severely practical and to examine some of the hard, inescapable facts and moral dilemmas which must face any government concerned to find the best possible balance between equity, adequacy and administrative efficiency. The fundamental ideological issues of socialist social policies and the private market are not, therefore, discussed here. Had this been my purpose I would have elaborated on my general conclusion. It is this. The challenge that faces us is not the choice between universalist and selective services. The real challenge resides in the question: what particular infrastructure of universalist services is needed in order to provide a framework of values and opportunity bases within and around which can be developed acceptable selective services provided, as social rights on criteria of the needs of specific categories, groups and territorial areas and not dependent on individual tests of means? It is in such practical ways which do not involve an assault on human dignity which are not socially divisive, and which do not lead to the development of two standards of services for two nations that more redistribution can be effected through the social services in favour of those whose needs are greatest.

There can therefore be no answer in Britain to the problems of poverty, ethnic integration, and social and educational inequalities without an infrastructure of universalist services. These are the essential foundations. We have to build on them and around them, face the hard, detailed challenge of how precisely to do so, and not run away in search of false gods or worn-out doctrines. Some of the answers have been hammered out and are known in Whitehall; what is now required is the courage to implement them.

R. M. Titmuss, *Commitment to Welfare* (1968), 114–23

74   Richard Crossman: A two-class health service, 1972

Crossman was Secretary of State for Social Services in the Labour government of 1966–70. Here he reflects on the nature of inequality within the health service.

In fact we are running a two-class system in the service. We are treating the patients in these long-stay hospitals (who are by the way half the inmates of our hospitals) as second-class citizens. Although they live there often for years and therefore need their creature comforts more, they are given less resources, less skills, less nursing staff, less food than those who have to spend ten days or three weeks in one of our luxury marble palaces. We, the healthy who go there for a short time and come out after the operation, are magnificently looked after. They who may spend the rest of their lives in these places are treated in an infinitely inferior way.

One of the virtues perhaps of being a minister is that one can see things which you who have seen them for so long fail to observe. What struck me as I went round and insisted on visiting the backward and bad hospitals as well as the good ones was the acceptance of inequality which had grown up in the health service. Many excuses were made to me. It wasn't worth doing anything for these poor people, I was told, because they ought not to be in those awful buildings and it would be a waste of money 'tarting up' wards that ought to be demolished. As for the indefensible contrast with the district hospital, they said that this is the kind of hospital people visit and go to themselves. When the service began in 1948 no doubt the founders believed that in the first ten years the inequality between the regions would be evened out and the inequality between the standard of living in the hospitals would be evened out. In fact they have not been evened out at all. I don't say of course that conditions haven't improved in the long-stay hospitals, but the gap between the money spent on them and what is spent in district hospitals is wider now than it was, owing to the inordinate cost of the new hospitals we are building and the higher standards we have in them.

R. H. S. Crossman, *A Politician's View of Health Service Planning* (Glasgow, 1972), 14–15

75   Sir George Godber and the process of policy formation, 1975

Godber was Chief Medical Officer of the Department of Health and Social Security. This account of the development of policy should be contrasted with that of Richard Crossman in the previous document.

I question whether it is possible to lay down precise plans for the levels of health care we hope to attain. The USSR, faced with a catastrophic situation in 1917, set up a closely integrated system in which policy and scale are closely defined at the centre. They had little choice in the face of disastrous epidemics, a desperate lack of doctors and social breakdown in the wake of universal service, accustomed over the years to central direction. Their pattern was such as Eastern Europe could adopt in similar conditions twenty-five years later and even China could use a similar system. It is not a pattern for us. We have achieved our own method of continuous modification, under central guidance but local decision and control. Progress is and must be evolutionary. The planning cycle of which we hear so much is a review of practical adjustments at annual intervals and it will succeed only to the extent that it carries conviction locally.

Sir George Godber, *Attainable Goals in Health* (Glasgow, 1976), 22

VI

The relationship between administration and policy

The administration of social policy is an important and vital subject, though not one which it is easy to illustrate with documents or to make exciting and attractive to students. It is important for at least two reasons. The practice of welfare is often influenced much more by the methods and perspectives of those who administer it than by the intentions and political rhetoric of those who introduced and passed the relevant legislation. The administrators need not necessarily share the political or ideological motives of the politicians and hence their interpretation of legislation may well differ from that of parliament. This would appear to be true at all levels of welfare administration, from those responsible for assisting ministers in drafting legislation to those responsible for exercising discretion vis-à-vis the individual recipient of welfare services or benefits. Accordingly, theory, intention and practice might vary to a greater or lesser degree (**69, 70**).

There is another important reason for studying the administration of welfare which was mentioned in the introduction. Over the years, there has been a considerable debate as to the extent of the independent role of civil servants in the development of social policy. Some writers have argued that the dynamic force behind changes in social policy is the civil service itself. It is civil servants who identify, establish and define social problems and who frame the only acceptable remedies for them. In this interpretation, 'bureaucratic imperatives' are important and the roles of politicians, pressure groups and outside forces generally are considered secondary (**61, 74, 75**).[1]

A powerful case can be made in support of this analysis but it does require very close examination. Supporting evidence would include several examples stretching from the regulation of conditions aboard emigrant ships in the early nineteenth century, carefully studied by MacDonagh, to the origins of the Butler Education Act of 1944, where it would appear that the initiative lay with the civil servants who were responsible for the administration of the pre-existing legislation (59).[2] Moreover, civil servants tend to consider themselves as very largely independent of outside pressures or, alternatively, as able to take a rather detached and balanced view of the conflicting forces. On the whole, it is very rarely that they will admit to bias in favour of one class or another in society, or even recognize the existence of antagonistic social classes. When they do, in a major crisis, it will usually be in terms of defending the national interest against extreme challenges from the left, or very occasionally from the right.[3]

These notions, that civil servants do hold the initiative and they are, to a great degree, independent of competing outside pressures, though sensitive to them, are of considerable interest, and they have been very important in conditioning the way in which the development of social policy has been conceived and interpreted by historians. But they cannot be taken at face-value because they do represent a peculiar ideological perspective. The origins of this view are to be traced back into the mid-nineteenth century when the role of the state in economic and social life is widely accepted as having reached a minimum under the influence of economic development and the analyses of the classical economists.

The reasons for the development of this peculiar ideology are extremely complex. They include changes in the social structure of Britain, with the emergence of numerically significant middle-class groups, divorced from the means of production (the demand at this stage for supervisory and management grades in industry was limited) and seeking a role in society. Relative independence from the necessity of seeking a living and limited opportunities in the traditional careers of the law and the church encouraged members to form and support a host of investigatory, charitable and welfare societies and to seek posts in the civil service at home and abroad. The popularity of rational or mechanical models of society enabled them to claim a hearing through their knowledge, increasingly quantitative, of the workings of society.[4] The experts and the civil servants reinforced each other's claims to status by reference to their skills and expertise and their ability to define and deal with social issues. This did not mean that there were not conflicts between the experts or within the civil service. There were, but these tended only to increase the attractiveness of such social roles (45–7).

In the eighteenth century, increasing awareness of the deficiencies of personal patronage and corruption had reinforced demands for a reduction in the role and size of government. Accordingly, in the nineteenth century, any extension of government activity required justification in terms of individualism – economic or social – or on utilitarian grounds. Bentham's famous dictum that 'all government is a great evil' continued, as J. Hart pointed out several years ago, 'nevertheless when by exercise of that evil a greater evil is prevented such action takes the name and character of good'.[5] Throughout the century departures from *laissez-faire* required and received support through the demonstration of their contribution to individual human welfare. As the size of welfare bureaucracies grew in the twentieth century the need for such justifications did not diminish as the ideology of *laissez-faire* retreated. Even today, massive bureaucracy is under attack from left and right, and indeed from many in the centre. The defence remains the unique ability of bureaucracy to preserve individual freedom and rights, a claim which is only now beginning to sound hollow from frequent repetition, and a growing perception of alternatives.

The implications of this analysis are far reaching and profound for the interpretation of the role of civil servants in the development of welfare. Most of the early historians of welfare were drawn from these strata of experts and civil servants. Pre-eminent, of course, were the Webbs, but there were many others, including W. H. Dawson, who wrote about the Bismarckian social insurance schemes in Germany, Beveridge, Schloss and Gilbert Slater.[6] Though often critical in their analyses, they tended to write from a centralist, establishment and civil service perspective, concentrating on the role of experts in the process of reform. They have been followed by a generation of academic historians, who also accepted this ideology, partly as a result of their own experience in the civil service, for example, during the second world war, and partly because they too desired to influence the direction of social policy. To be acceptable, influential and effective it was necessary for them to play 'the rules of the game'. Many of these writers, including R. M. Titmuss, who has been as great an influence on the historical writing of his students and their generation as the Webbs were in their time, were also critical of aspects of state welfare and aware of the implications of the views discussed here. But even Titmuss tended to suggest that welfare reform could be achieved by capturing intellectual control of the minds of the civil servants, perhaps reinforcing this by a little disciplined external pressure group activity to keep politicians and the media interested (73).[7]

Perhaps it is not surprising, therefore, that historians, even those who had little desire or inclination to seek changes in policy, have found it difficult to break out of the framework for the analysis of social policy which has been created. The weaknesses of alternative paradigms, such as the idea that reform is a reflex of working-class pressure, have contributed to the success of the current orthodoxy, but alone they do not explain it. The time has come to look critically at the role of the civil servants in the process of reform.

The traditional sources for research, however, help to reinforce the bias in favour of the central role of civil servants. The sheer bulk of the public archives, and the range of issues and interests which these records reflect, tends, almost inevitably, to encourage the belief that a serious and detailed study of their contents will reveal the vital and central processes of reform. The archives do contain the records of departmental policy formation and indications of pressure group activity. The latter is often subject to depreciating comment and criticism from the civil servants, which reinforces the impression that the latter were able to select freely from the proposals for reform which suited their own interests, concerns and perceptions.[8]

However, official sources tend to give less indication of the pre-shaping of opinion by the broader society or by social classes, the creation of what James Joll, in another context, called the 'unspoken assumptions'.[9] The pre-selection of the types of issue and forms of presentation which should be discussed or the way in which they were to be discussed comes out much less clearly from the public record. This does not mean, of course, that the civil servants did not often themselves play a role in selecting and shaping matters for discussion. The point being made here is that the issues were subjected to a form of selection, ordering and presentation which conditioned the views of the civil servants and this, often extremely subtle, process also requires investigation. For example in the 1920s and 1930s it seems clear that the overriding considerations affecting civil service discussions of changes in unemployment policy were the extent to which such changes would give rise to increased costs or create opportunities for abuse.[10] These were views which were not unique or original to the civil service, but were widely held and strongly urged by employers, representatives of the City and finance and Conservative politicians (30, 66).[11] Some elements of these attitudes had also been absorbed by some leading members of the Labour party. The effects of such changes in reducing poverty among the unemployed were also discussed, though seldom with the same weight accorded to them. The process by which humane, intelligent and caring people became conditioned to present and discuss social issues in this narrow and circumscribed framework is one which has never been satisfactorily analysed.

The influence of civil servants as administrators on the formation of social policy can be examined in various ways. Particular lines of policy can be followed through successive stages of evolution. This type of approach is perhaps the optimum for revealing the extent and limitations of civil service influence. It often indicates that popular, class or interest group pressure from outside was more significant in the origins of legislation but that, once the outlines of policy were laid down, the civil servants came into their own and had greater influence in subsequent modifications in that area of policy.[12] A detailed study of one area, however, is inappropriate in a work of this type and, accordingly, the rest of this chapter looks at a range of issues where expectations or historical analysis suggest that influence of administrators might be important. It cannot, however, be assumed that the extent of influence, or the lack of it, revealed here, in respect of any specific issue, necessarily reflects the importance of the civil servants at all times in that aspect of social policy.

In the late nineteenth century, the Poor Law was under increasing attack from without and subject to fissiparous tendencies within. Workers were less prepared to accept the workhouse or relief as a sufficient recompense for a lifetime of intermittent employment. Within and without the civil service there were two contrasting tendencies. Some Poor Law officials still believed that deficiencies in the Poor Law itself were to blame, and these could best be remedied by a return to the 'principles of 1834'. Such men as J. S. Davy seem to have intended to use the Royal Commission on the Poor Laws of 1905–9 as a means to this end.[13] Others, supported from outside pre-eminently by the Webbs, saw the answer in the continuing break-up of the Poor Law.[14] In this case, the solution adopted leant towards the latter, in that further agencies outside the Poor Law were created, but the impetus for reform came very largely from outside the civil service, though as has been indicated above, Morant, Llewellyn Smith, Beveridge and Braithwaite played their part (22–3, 39–44).[15]

One of the major breaches in the reliance on the Poor Law was the National Insurance Act of 1911. A direct consequence of this act was the discovery and preliminary quantification of the extent of illness among women in employment, covered by Part I, the health insurance section (65). The extent of illness among women had implications for effectiveness of the act as a whole, since women and children as dependants were excluded from benefits. Yet despite the increasing knowledge of female illness, despite the large influx of women into the labour market during the first and second world wars, it was not until 1948 that women and children obtained coverage, as dependants, under national insurance. The administrators had provided the information and the knowledge but reform did not follow.

During the 1920s the administration of unemployment insurance during periods of mass unemployment was shaped by attitudes which seem somewhat inappropriate in retrospect (**69, 70**). Reinforcing this was the 'Treasury view' of public expenditure which helped stifle any initiative in regard to reform. However, though changes in the administration of unemployment insurance did occur in the 1920s and 1930s, the development of new approaches to the problem of unemployment was linked to the administrative process in a curious and tangential way.

The idea that public expenditure had to be restrained for the benefit of the economy, and to keep down the level of unemployment by preventing the misdirection of scarce resources, was not unique to the civil service and the Treasury. Employers and their organizations took a very similar view. As a result of pressure from the latter a series of new institutions was created including the Unemployment Insurance Statutory Committee of 1934, charged with overseeing and curtailing the level of expenditure on benefits and the Economic Advisory Council, a much denigrated body which was intended to produce new ideas on the problems facing the British economy. Employers hoped that these new institutions would control public expenditure and support plans for the restructuring of British industry. Paradoxically, both these bodies provided a forum for discussions between employers, experts – in this case pre-eminently economists – and civil servants, which contributed in the end to the formation of a new positive attitude to the role of public expenditure and social services, in particular, in the development of the economy. Keynes's analysis of the nature and causes of cyclical unemployment and his suggested remedies were, in part, a response to the debates within the Economic Advisory Council.[16]

As this example shows, the relationship between administration and the development of policy is extremely complex, with the initiative passing back and forward between administrators, experts and social groups or classes. Since the second world war, a similar interaction of forces can be observed, though a novel feature is the emergence of a series of pressure groups representing particular sections of society whose needs are not being met within the existing welfare system, such as the Child Poverty Action Group, Shelter and Age Concern. These groups have operated on two levels. They have pressed for improved administration to ensure that the eligible persons receive the benefits to which they are entitled. Many existing benefits have relatively low take-up rates. They have also campaigned for new legislation to provide for those not covered by current benefits. It is true that some innovations in policy have originated within the departments concerned but, as far as can be judged from the published sources, it has been more common for the civil service to react to outside pressures of various kinds. The 'wage-stop', a system of limiting social security benefits to levels below that of the wages the claimant was receiving prior to his application, was ended – it appears – very largely as the result of a change of government and pressure from outside experts. Such judgements remain provisional, of course, until the relevant documents become available for study.

All in all, while the study of administrative processes does reveal much about the on-going amendment of official policy on social issues, it is dangerous to take at face-value the estimates of influence of politicians and civil servants involved therein. Major shifts of policy seem to occur more as the result of an interaction between internal developments and the pressure of the dominant material forces in British society. In studying welfare in practice it is not sufficient to concentrate on the documents at the centre or the texts of the acts which relate to social issues. The social context of welfare policy is vital and hence the attitudes, intentions and influence of those groups and classes in society in a position to affect that policy have to be understood and explained. The development of the welfare state in Britain since the 1880s is a complex social process which reveals a great deal about the nature of British society. For this reason alone it is essential that it is not studied in isolation.

NOTES

1 O. MacDonagh, *A Pattern of Goverment Growth: The Passenger Acts and Their Enforcement, 1800–60* (1961); D. Roberts, *The Victorian Origins of the British Welfare State* (New Haven, 1960); R. Davidson, 'Llewellyn Smith, the Labour Department and Government Growth', in G. Sutherland (ed.), *Studies in the Growth of Nineteenth-Century Government* (1972).

2 P. H. J. H. Gosden, *Education in the Second World War* (1977); R. A. Butler, *The Art of the Possible* (1973 edn), 93–4. Even here the effects of evacuation and pressure from religious leaders for equality opportunity in education were important in starting the process.

3 J. R. Hay, 'Government Policy towards Labour in Britain, 1900–14', *Scottish Labour History Society Journal* 10 (1976), 41–9.

4 O. R. MacGregor, 'Social Research and Social Policy in the Nineteenth Century', *British Journal of Sociology* 8 (1957).

5 J. Hart, 'Nineteenth-Century Social Reforms: a Tory Interpretation of History', *Past and Present* 31 (1965).

6 W. H. Dawson, *Social Insurance in Germany, 1883–1911* (1912); W. H. Beveridge, *Unemployment: a Problem of Industry* (1909); D. F. Schloss, *Insurance against Unemployment* (1909); G. Slater, *Poverty and the State* (1930).

7 R. M. Titmuss, *Commitment to Welfare* (1968).

8 W. H. Beveridge, *Power and Influence* (1953); H. N. Bunbury (ed.), *Lloyd George's Ambulance Wagon: Being the Memoirs of William J. Braithwaite, 1911–12* (1957); see also V. G. Kiernan, *Marxism and Imperialism* (1974), 76.

9 J. Joll, '1914: The Unspoken Assumptions', in H. W. Koch (ed.), *The Origins of the First World War* (1972).

10 A. Deacon, *In Search of the Scrounger* (1976).

11 Peter K. Cline, 'Eric Geddes and the "Experiment" with Businessmen in Government, 1915–22', in K. D. Brown (ed.), *Essays in Anti-Labour History* (1974), 74–104.

12 For an excellent study of this type, see J. Harris, *Unemployment and Politics, 1886–1914* (Oxford, 1972).

13 At least according to Beatrice Webb, *Our Partnership* (1948), 317.

14 Even Walter Long, the Conservative President of the Local Government Board in 1904, seems to have had in mind a move away from the Poor Law (43, 64).

15 See, for fuller discussion, J. R. Hay, *The Origins of the Liberal Welfare Reforms, 1906–14* (1975), 25–42.

16 S. Howson and D. Winch, *The Economic Advisory Council* (Cambridge, 1977).

Further reading

There is a vast literature on the welfare state in Britain. The following list is a brief selection to supplement the works mentioned in the text. Place of publication is London unless otherwise stated.

Documentary collections

M. Bruce, *The Rise of the Welfare State: English Social Policy, 1601–1971*, 1973.

E. Butterworth and R. Holman, *Social Welfare in Modern Britain*, 1975.

M. E. Rose, *The English Poor Law, 1780–1930*, Newton Abbot, 1971.

B. Watkin, *Documents on Health and Social Services, 1834 to the Present Day*, 1975.

General studies

M. Bruce, *The Coming of the Welfare State*, 3rd edn., 1966.

D. Fraser, *The Evolution of the British Welfare State*, 1973.

V. George, *Social Security and Society*, 1973.

T. H. Marshall, *Social Policy*, 2nd edn., 1967.

M. E. Rose, *The Relief of Poverty, 1834–1914*, 1972.

J. F. Sleeman, *The Welfare State: its Aims, Benefits and Costs*, 1973.

R. M. Titmuss, *Essays on the Welfare State*, 1963.

Themes and topics

A. Briggs, 'The Welfare State in Historical Perspective', *Archives Européennes de Sociologie* 2, 1961.

K. D. Brown, *Labour and Unemployment, 1900–14*, Newton Abbot, 1971.

V. George, *Social Security: Beveridge and After*, 1968.

B. B. Gilbert, *The Evolution of National Insurance*, 1966.

B. B. Gilbert, *British Social Policy, 1914–39*, 1970.

P. Hall, H. Land, R. Parker and A. Webb, *Change, Choice and Conflict in Social Policy*, 1975.

J. F. Harris, *Unemployment and Politics, 1886–1914*, Oxford, 1972.

J. F. Harris, *William Beveridge*, Oxford, 1977.

J. R. Hay, *The Origins of the Liberal Welfare Reforms, 1906–14*, 1975.

J. C. Kincaid, *Poverty and Equality in Britain*, 1973.

R. Pinker, *Social Theory and Social Policy*, 1971.

G. V. Rimlinger, *Welfare Policy and Industrialization in Europe, America and Russia*, New York, 1971.

W. A. Robson, *Welfare State and Welfare Society: Illusion and Reality*, 1976.

J. Stevenson, *Social Conditions in Britain Between the Wars*, 1977.

R. M. Titmuss, *Problems of Social Policy*, 1950.

D. Wedderburn, 'Facts and Theories of the Welfare State', in R. Miliband and J. Saville (eds), *The Socialist Register*, 1965.

Index